TINY HOUSE LIVING

RV Living

&

Shipping Container Homes

Bill Oatfield

© **Copyright 2020 by Bill Oatfield – All rights reserved.**

In no way is it legal to reproduce, duplicate, or transmit any part of this document in either electronic means or in printed format. Recording of this publication is strictly prohibited and any storage of this document is not allowed unless with written permission from the publisher.

The information provided herein is stated to be truthful and consistent, in that any liability, in terms of inattention or otherwise, by any usage or abuse of any policies, processes, or directions contained within is the solitary and utter responsibility of the recipient reader. Under no circumstances will any legal responsibility or blame be held against the author for any reparation, damages, or monetary loss due to the information herein, either directly or indirectly.

The information herein is offered for informational purposes solely, and is universal as so. The presentation of the information is without contract or any type of guarantee assurance.

Legal Disclaimer: all photos used in this book are published on Flickr.com under the Attribution 2.0 Generic (CC BY 2.0) license.

REVIEWS

Reviews and feedback help improve this book and the author.

If you enjoy this book, we would greatly appreciate it if you were able to take a few moments to share your opinion and post a review online.

Table of Contents

BOOK 1 – RV LIVING: A Beginner's Guide To Turning Your Motorhome Dream Into Reality

Introduction..14

1. Choosing The Right RV For You....................18
    Class A
    Class B
    Class C

2. New Or Used? That's The Question..............28
    Deciding on Buying a New or Used Rv
    Dealerships
    RV Shows

3. What To Look For When Checking Out An RV..36
    Why You Need to Test the Systems of an RV
    Water System
    Electrical System
    Propane System
    Other Things to Check
    Get Roadside Assistance

4. How To Finance The Purchase Of An RV.....50
    Be Prepared to Haggle
    How to Get a Loan
    Know Your Credit Score
    Mistakes to Avoid When Getting a Loan

5. Preparing For RV Living.....58
    Choosing a Domicile State
    How to Get a Permanent Address
    Set up Electronic Deliveries
    Set up a Digital Signature
    Use the Campsite Address
    Use the Local Post Office Address
    Voting
    Medical Care
    Jury Duty

6. How To Budget For The Road.....74
    Budget: Where to Start?
    How to Save Money
    Finding a Job on the Road
    Finding an Online Source of Income
    Blogging
    Selling on Amazon
    Drop shipping
    Teaching English
    Freelancing

7. Getting Along In An RV.....92

  Make Sure Your RV Has Enough Room
  Choose a Sturdy RV
  Assign Roles
  Respect Each Other's Storage Space
  Assign a Place For Your Pet
  Avoid Clutter
  Do Not Travel Too Much in One Day
  Stick to Your Budget
  Communicate Openly

8. Finding The Best Campgrounds, Paid Or Not..102
  What is Boondocking
  Apps for Boondocking
  Campground Sites Memberships

9. RV Resources..112
  RV Lifestyle Websites
  RV Lifestyle Apps
  Finding Campsites Websites
  Making Money Online Websites
  Memberships Websites
  Roadside Assistance Websites

Conclusion...118

BOOK 2 – SHIPPING CONTAINER HOMES: Learn How To Build Your Own Shipping Container House and Live Your Dream!

Introduction..122

1. What Are Shipping Container Homes?..126
    Turning a Shipping Container Into a Home
    How Shipping Containers Are Used For Retail and Housing

2. The Benefits of Shipping Container Homes..136
    Shipping Containers Are Cheap
    Shipping Containers are Sturdy
    Shipping Containers are Widely Available
    Shipping Containers are Eco-Friendly
    Shipping Containers Can Be Ready For Use Quickly
    Shipping Containers Offer Design Creativity and Flexibility

3. What to Consider Before Purchasing a Shipping Container..150
    Used Shipping Containers Could Contain Toxic Chemicals
    Budget for Insulation

Educate Yourself on Local Building/Safety Regulations

4. Choosing the Right Shipping Container..158

Shipping Container Sizes
What Does a Shipping Container Cost?
Other Costs to Take Into Account
Prefabricated Shipping Container Homes

5. Are Shipping Container Homes Safe?..174

Used Shipping Containers Are Coated With Harmful Chemicals
Container Floors Are Treated With Pesticides
What Can You Do To Remove These Chemicals?
Laying a Solid Foundation
Indoor Safety Precautions

6. How To Design A Shipping Container Home...186

Hire a Pro
Choose the Right Foundation
Floor Plans
Floor Selection
Plumbing Work
Electrical Wiring
Temperature and Noise Insulation
Use the Right Toolset

Consider a Hip Roof

7. Where To Purchase A Shipping Container..202
Start Online
Ask Family and Friends
Inspection: What to Look Out For?
The Moment is There: Let's Buy That Shipping Container!

8. Building Permit and Other Legal Requirements...214
What is a Building Code?
Rules Vary Per Region
Research Different Locations
Hire a Local Architect
Prepare all the Paperwork
Address Specific Concerns Regarding Shipping Containers
Communicate Openly

9. Final Considerations..................................226
Living in an Eco-Friendly Way
Family
Downsizing
Join the Community

Conclusion..234

About The Author..238

BOOK 1 – RV LIVING: A Beginner's Guide To Turning Your Motorhome Dream Into Reality

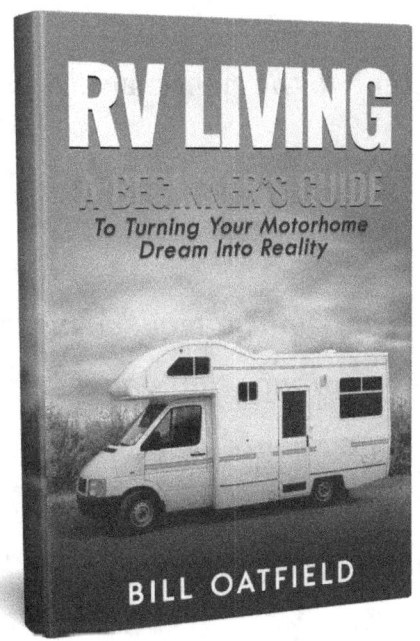

Introduction

Thank you for purchasing this book, *'RV Living: A Beginner's Guide To Turning Your Motorhome Dream Into Reality'*. Clearly, you have an interest in understanding what truly goes into living full-time, or even part-time, in a motorhome.

And you have come to the right place!

It was Mark Twain who said:

"Twenty years from now you will be more disappointed by the things that you didn't do than by the ones you did do. So throw off the bowlines. Sail away from the safe harbor. Catch the trade winds in your sails. Explore. Dream. Discover."

With choosing to live in a recreational vehicle, or RV, you are doing exactly that.

RV living is essentially living in a recreational vehicle full-time, like you would in an apartment or a house.

The most common recreational vehicle many think of is an RV camper, which houses all of the amenities of home within the confines of a bus. Many RV campers come with lavish looks on the inside as well as pertinent designs on the outside, but a lot of those will cost a good deal of cash up front. This book will address the many ways in which you can purchase an RV, as well as how to get the best bang for your buck when it comes to the quality of your potential RV camper.

This book covers all facets of RV living, from how to cope with living in close proximity to your loved ones all the way to handling your mail and doctors appointments. This comprehensive book on RV living will teach you how to budget your money, make money while on the road, cover extra expenses and accessories that come with RV living, as well as guide you through the process of choosing the perfect recreational vehicle for you and your loved ones.

However, RV living is not just comprised of purchasing a vehicle and coming up with a budget. There are also other facets to navigate, like residing in such close proximity with other adults and possibly even pets, how to save money on the road, and how to work (if necessary) while you are traveling. All of these things come into question at some point in time whenever someone is traveling full-time in an RV, and they are legitimate questions that will be answered within the walls of this book.

When you finish this book, not only will you know if living in a recreational vehicle is something you wish to do, but you will have all of the basics at your disposal so you can navigate this new and adventurous lifestyle with ease and confidence.

Now is the day on which you can take the **first step** to **changing your life**.

Thank you for purchasing this book, and I hope you find it to be the best resource you could possibly have on RV living.

Welcome to the RV family!

1. Choosing The Right RV For You

"I got it one piece at a time
And it didn't cost me a dime
You'll know it's me when I come through your town
I'm gonna ride around in style
I'm gonna drive everybody wild
'Cause I'll have the only one there is around"

One Piece At A Time – Johnny Cash

Key Takeaway: *There are three classes of RVs: A, B, and C. Each have their own upsides and downsides, but the most popular class for many beginning full-time RV residents is Class C.*

When a living space and an engine are combined into one vehicle, it is called a motorhome. The more common phrase is "RV," and it is designated today as a permanent living space for many individuals. No matter the type of motorhome you wish to choose for your particular situation, they all fall into three different classes: A, B, and C.

***

Class A

Class As are the largest motorhomes, with lengths and widths up to that of a tour bus. If you picture a Greyhound bus, you have an idea of how large one of these things is.

Example of a Class A RV

Many relish over these RVs because of the space inside as well as the amenities at their disposal. These motorhomes usually have lavish decorations inside to make the interior space seem more like a traditional house, but as the amenities and interior beauty escalate, so does the price. Some used ones can be found for as cheap as $60,000, while many that are outfitted and brand new can cost someone up to millions of dollars, depending on how they wish to outfit it.

Class A motorhomes can be up to 45 feet long, which give the RV dwellers ample room, and part of that space is usually used for a master suite as well as a full-sized bathroom and shower. Some can come preinstalled with their own washer and dryer unit, and come decked out with multiple sliders that can expand the width of the bus by 14-feet. It is the most customizable motorhome with some of the add-ons being an ice machine, a flat-screen television, and a dishwasher, not to mention all of the storage space that comes with it.

However, everything has a downside, and Class A motorhomes are no different. Fuel economy is slim-to-none with a vehicle like this, with the average gas mileage being somewhere between 9-12 miles per gallon. Another downside to a motorhome like this is the necessity for a toad, which is a separate vehicle that comes along with the travel. When you set up camp in something as big as this, it becomes impractical to constantly pack it up and drive every time someone needs to run into town for an appointment or food. This means maintaining two vehicles that are constantly on the road.

***

Class B

Then there are the Class B motorhomes, which are simply campervans.

Example of a Class B RV

This is the smallest motorhome class, but many people have been known to outfit them with lavish interiors, making them incredibly comfortable and livable. For an individual who wants to travel a great deal with their RV, this is the most affordable option. The price ranges from $40,000 to $80,000 while still coming with all of the basic amenities a living situation needs: a bed area, a sink, a stove top, and a refrigerator.

They do still have some storage, though not nearly as much as the other two classes, and are most popular among single individuals who do not understand how to work a tow hitch.

The size variance is the greatest on a Class B motorhome. They lack the over-cab portion that a Class C motorhome provides (see below), but the utilization of a cargo van base means the size can range from a standard full-sized cargo van all the way to a 20-foot vehicle.

Some of the plus sides to this type of RV are the gas mileage (18-20 miles per gallon!), the ease of maneuverability, and the fact that many standard Class B motorhomes can fit into a standard garage and a mall parking space.

However, this class does have drastic downsides: there is no master suite, so the bed is usually a drop-down table or a fold-out couch. There is also not much space, so maneuvering within the motorhome will be difficult. And the entertainment afforded to someone utilizing the space within this class of motorhome is either a radio or a small-screen television.

***

Class C

Class Cs are what many consider "typical motorhomes." They have a normal chassis (the base frame for the motor vehicle) and a bunking situation above the cab

Example of a Class C RV

Their length ranges anywhere between 20 and 33 feet, and the front looks like a normal van or pickup truck, with the RV's body extending over the cab where the driver and passenger dwell during travel. This extended space above the cab is the sleeping space, and this area can easily fit a queen or king-sized bed, making it very comfortable for two individuals. They are much smaller than a Class A motorhome, but they do not lack in space. What it loses in elongated space it makes up for in interior compartments.

Space in a Class C is also utilized better, with many storage compartments on the outside to store things such as portable grills, televisions, and sewer hoses. Plus, with the smaller length of the motorhome, it is much easier to maneuver down the road and in motorhome parks. This class of motorhome can have a price tag of anywhere between $45,000 to $140,000.

Another upside to going with a Class C motorhome is the fact that a service and warranty work is easier to come by. Because the driving portion of the motorhome usually has a brand name cab and a drive train, many auto dealers cannot turn around and claim ignorance on how to service the vehicle. Plus, with the diminished size from a Class A motorhome, many more camping ground opportunities become available for you to utilize. The gas mileage is a bit better compared to a Class A, but you will still only get around 15 miles to the gallon in a Class C motorhome.

Yet, as with everything else, there are downsides: there aren't many slide out options for a Class C motorhome, so expanding the width of the RV is not an option. Plus, when your RV needs to have maintenance work performed on it, if you aren't attempting to do it yourself, then you will end up losing your entire home for the duration of the service time. However, the same is true for the RVs in the other two classes.

***

Now you know the differences between a Class A, B and C RV motorhome.

For most people, a Class C RV would be the best option. If you are on a budget, and don't mind getting cozy in a small space a lot, you may want to consider a Class B Rv. And if price isn't an issue, and you are comfortable riding a vehicle the size of a bus, then a Class A RV is your go-to motorhome!

Once you have decided which class best fits your needs and wants, the following pressing question arises: should you buy a new or used RV?

That is what we will cover next.

2. New Or Used? That's The Question

"I see my path, but I don't know where it leads. Not knowing where I'm going is what inspires me to travel it."

Rosalia de Castro

Key Takeaway: Purchasing an RV can be an intimidating process for a first-timer. The more you learn about RVs prior to any purchase decision, the better. You will better understand your own likes and dislikes, you will know what to avoid, and you will be able to leverage your expertise when negotiating price. Start with reading up on RVs. And then get your feet wet by visiting local dealerships and possibly an RV show. You are not going to know what coffee tastes like if you only read books about it, right? It is the same with getting a feel for RVs.

What is most intimidating for many first-time (potential) RV owners is the actual purchasing process. Many don't know whether to go new or used, whether to pay cash or finance, and many do not understand the basic elements to look at before committing to purchasing an RV.

The short version is:

- Buy a new RV, and your main concern is going to be how to finance it.
- Buy a used RV, and your main concern is going to be not buying a pig in a poke.

In any case, you can save yourself a lot of future headaches if you make an informed decision now. The more you educate yourself about RVs beforehand, the better you will know what you want and expect from an RV, and what you will need to look out for.

***

Deciding on Buying a New or Used Rv

To get an idea what to look for when buying an RV, the best thing to do is to take a look at a couple of RVs first, and pick an expert's brain. Sure, you can learn a lot from books like this or watching explainer videos online. But that is not enough. You will only get a real feel for what to look for when buying an RV if you have seen and touched a bunch. In person.

Just like purchasing a regular car, you will always get a better deal buying from an individual than from a dealership. However, first-time buyers would benefit from a trip to a dealership, if only to pick the salesman's brain about the vehicle as a whole. Remember, we are not buying yet. We are simply orienting ourselves on what is on the market.

So where do you go to when you want to take a look at the various RVs on the market?

These are your two best options:

- Local Dealerships
- RV Shows

Make sure you have a decent understanding of RVs before your visit, so you know the right questions to ask! Read this book, and check out websites and Youtube videos on RV living. After you have done that, you can be confident that you have a solid level of knowledge, decent enough to make a visit to a local dealer or RV show worthwhile.

***

Dealerships

There are a ton of RV dealers out there. Unless you are living in a very remote area, you will definitely be able to find a local RV dealer.

These dealers have a great variety of motorhomes at display. Like car salesmen, they get paid commission on their sales. But no one expects you to buy an RV on the spot at your first visit. Regardless of the class you are interested in, purchasing an RV is a big financial investment. A wise (wo)man will first want to do due diligence before committing to such a purchase. And RV dealers understand this. If you do feel pressured into making a purchase decision on the spot, take a breath and keep your guard up. This is your money we are talking about. Spend it wisely, and only after enough deliberation.

With that said, feel free to take a look at their showroom, and pick the brains of the person that is showing you around. Take notes on anything that catches your attention. You may want to do further research when you come home. And do not forget to bring your camera and take a lot of pictures!

***

RV Shows

Attending an RV show is another excellent way of checking out the many different motorhomes that are on offer. These are big events, with performances, live music and of course many RVs at display. Check out the calendar of the Recreational Vehicle Industry

Association (RVIA), rvia.org, to find one near you. Most shows are organized in spring, summer and fall.

There will be many more motorhomes that you can check out at an RV show, compared to visiting a dealership. Also, a dealership often has an exclusive relationship with a particular brand. This means that you will only be able to see RVs from a particular brand at that particular dealership. Finally, you will find representatives of both dealers and manufacturers at RV shows. So if one person cannot answer your question, you can just walk to the next booth and ask it to someone else!

The downside of an RV show is that you cannot visit them year round. Unless you want to book a flight ticket, you will have to wait until an RV show is organized in a city near you. It would be best to first visit a dealership, and then attend an RV show later on.

Keep in mind that RV shows are also full of salesmen, looking to close a deal. Like when visiting a dealership, make sure you have your wits about you. Before you even walk into the venue, decide whether you are willing to buy an RV today or not. Stick to that decision, no matter what! Keep in mind that your main reason for being at this show is to learn more about the different types of RVs on the market. This knowledge will help you to make a more informed decision later on. Plus, you will be able to leverage your expertise when negotiating price.

***

That is how you can get an idea of the different types of RVs that are on the market, so you can make an informed decision on what you want, and whether to buy a new or used RV.

Next up, we'll discuss what to look for when testing an RV, so you can buy the best RV for you.

3. What To Look For When Checking Out An RV

"Brrrm brm brm brm brm brm brrrm
Brrrm brm brm brm brm brm brrrm

Take me riding in the car, car
Take me riding in the car, car"

Riding in my Car – Woody Guthrie

<u>Key Takeaway</u>: *Testing an RV's systems is the most important thing you will need to do prior to purchasing it. This is why it is crucial you first educate yourself on RVs. If you do not feel comfortable testing the systems of the vehicle you are interested in on your own, hire an expert. The main systems you will need to check are the water, electrical and propane systems.*

The biggest piece of advice is to never purchase an RV without testing every single system first.

In this chapter, you will learn why this is so important, and which systems you will need to test.

***

Why You Need to Test the Systems of an RV

You have to make sure that every single system works and has been maintained the way it needs to be. Whether you are purchasing new or used, making sure all of the systems are tested is necessary. The last thing you want to be stuck with is an RV whose systems begin to break down one week into your new journey.

If you want to check these systems yourself, you will need a:

- Water hose
- Charged car battery
- Cigarette lighter power adapter
- Charger to plug into that adapter

- Normal wall outlet adapter
- Regular propane cylinder, and a
- Truck with a towing package (only if you are looking at a motorhome that tows behind your vehicle)

If you are uncomfortable with testing the systems yourself, it is wise to bring in someone to test them for you. This will cost you around $180 to $300. However, if things are found wrong with the RV before negotiations begin taking place, that can be used as a real bargaining chip when agreeing on price. Not to mention the money you keep in your pocket if you decide to call the whole thing off.

How do you test the systems? This process is not as overwhelming as it feels if you take it one step at a time. Purchasing an RV does not happen in a day, and if you span the process over the course of even a week, you will feel much better about your purchase over all.

***

Water System

In order to test the water system, you need to hook the hose you brought with you up to the water intake line of the RV and then hook the other one up to some sort of running water outside the RV. This is what it means to be "hooked up," but some people refer to it as being on "city water."

Once this hookup is complete and you have determined that water is flowing into the RV, then begin turning on faucets, shower heads, and flushing the toilet. Make sure all of these things flow efficiently and disperse water the way they should. In order to gauge the water pressure, turn the outside spigot on before hooking up the hose. Whatever that water pressure is, should be the water pressure for the inside of the RV.

Then, leave the water running slowly out of one of the faucets, then shut everything else down. Go outside and find the sewer outlet, and while you are bending over to find it, check underneath the RV. Make sure there are no leaks or spillage of any sort. Then, as a check, drain the water from the RV to make sure there is no black water, or water that is dirtied or contaminated in any way from the RV. Keep in mind throughout the draining process to make sure there is no leakage anywhere.

After this, one more water test remains: checking the water pump. To do this, you need to locate the RV's fresh water storage tank. Fill it with water and then remove the hose hookup from the "city water." Then, find the switch to turn on the water pump and listen to it. If there is a lot of noise or shaking (some noise will happen depending on the model, but it should not roar) it means the water pump will need to be replaced soon, and that can be used as another bargaining chip when coming to a reasonable price-point. But, when you have the water pump turned on, try the faucets yet again and check the water pressure that is instituted by the water pump. Then, go back outside and check for leaks near the water pump. If you can get through with no issues and leaks, then your water system in the RV is ready to go!

***

Electrical System

Then, there is the electrical system to test. Most RVs run directly off a 12-volt battery, which is the equivalent of a car or marine battery. But, they also (usually) have the capability to plug into a 30-amp or 50-amp system at an RV park. For both of these power sources, there will be two separate breakers. The 12-volt battery controls most of the internal indicators and lights, as well as the refrigerator unit in the RV. Everything else usually runs off the hook up at the RV park you dock at.

For testing the 12-volt system, connect a good battery to the RV and begin turning on internal RV lights and indicators. Make sure they work. Plug in the cigarette charger adaptor and plug something in. Make sure that works as well. If they are not working, the first thing to do is to check the fuses in the fusebox, then check to make sure the battery you are using has enough juice in it.

Once you can make sure all of this is good to go, then plug the RV's external power cable into a source of electricity. Most RVs have a plug that is a three-prong setup, so if you want to connect it to a basic wall outlet you might need an adaptor. Make sure the breaker in the box is turned on, and then check to make sure the rest of the internal appliances work properly. Plug a phone charger directly into a wall outlet in the RV and see if it will charge the phone, and remember to check the lights again in the RV. They should work no matter what power source the vehicle is hooked up to. Again, if nothing is working, check the breaker box to make sure no switches have been flipped. But, if everything works, then this system test is done as well!

***

Propane System

Then, testing the propane system is next. This is the final major component of the RV's system, and this is what fuels the stovetop, any additional heaters, the refrigerator's backup system, and the hot water heater. In order to test this, find where the propane cylinders are and switch it out for the one you brought. Propane lines screw left for tightness and right for looseness, which is the opposite of everything else. Once you have the line connected to your filled propane cylinder, twist the nozzle on top of your cylinder. When you hear the short hiss, the propane will begin to fill the lines of the RV.

Then, the testing begins. Go into the RV and turn on a burner, then light a match. If the propane is making it through the lines, the propane should catch the match, therefore heating the burner just as any home gas stove would. Make sure to test all of the stovetop burners in this fashion.

For the oven, there is usually a pilot light that needs to be lit in order to test it. But, the test for the oven is the same way for the stoves.

Once you have those tested, go outside and unplug your outer power cable. Then, look at the control panel on the refrigerator. Find the "auto" setting if there is one, and if not, then look for the "gas" and "lp" toggle on it. Either way, flip it to make sure the refrigerator is now running off the propane source. Listen closely. If you hear any sort of clicking sound that extends for a long period of time or any sort of "check" light clicks itself on, then you have an issue with the backup system to the refrigerator. But, if you do not, stick around until you feel some sort of elemental change inside the refrigerator.

Then, it's off to the water heater tank. Follow the individual instructions to light it and get it going, and then go inside and turn on a hot water faucet. Wait until there is hot water coming out.

Once you have verified that all of these components are working properly and have been tested, then the RV has no issues with its major systems! Keep in mind, you still have to get the RV inspected, but this means the RV is good for purchase if you don't wish to inherit any issues.

***

Other Things to Check

Other things to keep in mind that enhance living in a recreational vehicle are things like cable hookups in order to test the television and cable outlet and built-in radios and DVD players that will need to be tested as well. However, in all of the testing of the "fun things," do not forget to test the RV's more important features, like the frame and roof. Make sure things are solid, free of damage, and unwavering. For the roof, a typical RV should be able to support one solid person with no issues of bending or wavering. If the roof is squishy or soggy, that is a massive issue to deal with.

Also, give the tires a good kick. Check the brakes and the fluids in the vehicle, and ask the seller how long the vehicle has been sitting. When checking the brakes, listen out for a noise inside of the tires. This indicates that the electrical brakes are working the way they should. If you do not hear that sound, address it immediately. Also, check the axles and make sure no major damage has been issued to them. Make sure the motorhome is sitting level, both front to back and side to side, when sitting stationary on level ground. If all of this seems intimidating, many garages will have someone that will accompany you to look over the RV at an hourly rate (which spans anywhere between $25-$75 an hour).

Testing the systems yourself before bringing in an inspector is imperative. While inspectors will give it an overall look, their job is not to test every facet of every system. Their job is to make sure nothing major is damaged so that you will be safe on the road.

This means checking the mechanisms under the hood, giving the engine a good look, testing the lights, checking the windshield wipers, and making sure nothing major is leaking. If the test is done to a car for inspection, it will be done to the RV. However, that leaves a lot to be desired. The inspection is required simply to prove to your insurance company insuring the vehicle that it is approved to run safely on the road.

That does not mean its system will be in tip-top shape.

***

Get Roadside Assistance

Finally, please understand: no matter what RV you choose to buy, and no matter if you choose new or used, always have dependable roadside assistance. Always. Things will happen on the road when a vehicle like this is being run to its limits, and even though the vehicle is created to handle the rough and rugged terrain of many different types of environments, it means there are higher chances of something going wrong while on the road.

Why?

Because that is the environment the vehicle is living in! Just like there is a higher percentage of rust with cars in states that salt their roads heavily during the winter months, there is a higher percentage of something happening to your vehicle while on the road because that is the vehicle's dominant environment.

These are some of the companies that offer roadside assistance:

- Good Sam (Goodsamroadside.com)
- Coach-Net (Coach-Net.com)
- Progressive (Progressive.com)

Pay a little money upfront, and save yourself a lot of money and trouble later on!

***

If the RV passes all your main systems checks, you are no longer shooting in the dark. If you decide to go ahead with the purchase, you can be confident that this motorhome is going to give you years of pleasure on the road!

Buying an RV is not cheap though. If you are like most people, you will probably need to finance at least part of the purchase price. How you would go about financing the purchase of your dream RV is what you will learn in the following chapter.

4. How To Finance The Purchase Of An RV

"A budget tells us what we can't afford, but it doesn't keep us from buying it."

William Feather

Key Takeaway: *Whether you are considering a new or used one, purchasing an RV motorhome requires a serious financial investment. Be prepared to haggle down the price. And if you are going to take out a loan, be smart about it. Know your credit score, shop around, and know what you can afford.*

When buying an RV, your safest bet is a new one. It just rolled out of the factory and has never been used. Moreover, you can expect the latest and greatest in terms of design and motor parts.

High quality comes at a price though. How you are going to finance the purchase?

Because a new RV requires a bigger financial investment, the advice in this chapter is mostly tailored to this situation. However, most of it applies equally to purchasing a used RV.

***

Be Prepared to Haggle

First off, when financing an RV, keep in mind that many RV salesmen expect you to haggle on the price. Many RVs on the lots are marked up as much as 30% from the suggested retail price, so do not be intimidated to ask for a lower price than the ticket price on the vehicle.

***

How to Get a Loan

If financing is the way to go for you, there are some things to keep in mind: try to find someone outside the dealership that will loan you the money. RV dealerships are middlemen between you and the bank, meaning they usually have a contract with the original loan agency to have a cut of every loan they dole out from their dealership. To avoid dealer markup, go straight to the loaning agency you wish to work with beforehand.

Another thing to keep in mind is considering putting some form of money down when dealing with the lending institution. The more financial risk you take on personally, the more willing they are to not simply give you a loan, but to give you a better interest rate.

Like when finding your dream RV, I encourage you to shop around a bit first. Make a few appointments with different banks to familiarize yourself with the terms, and use online tools to compare terms to figure out the best deal for your situation.

***

Know Your Credit Score

Also, just like a car loan, your credit score will be taken into consideration when obtaining a loan, as well as with the interest rate of the loan. Make sure to be familiar with yours before going in. And, just like a car, the original ticket price does not include things such as taxes, fees, and additional add-ons.

Your credit history is also checked when applying for an RV loan, so not only does your credit score come into play, but so does your payment history and any other debt you currently have. But rest assured: even those with a lower credit score can still get a loan for an RV if they go through the dealership, just be ready for a markup and a higher interest rate overall.

If it is possible, try to pay as much up front as possible. New RVs depreciate in value as much as 30% when someone drives it off the lot, so you will always owe significantly more on it than it is worth. But, if you pay some up front, like a down payment on a car, then you can avoid the type of heartache that comes with totaling an RV and not getting enough back from the insurance company to pay off the loan.

***

Mistakes to Avoid When Getting a Loan

You already learned that you need to be willing to negotiate the purchase price down. Any dollar you are not paying, you don't have to borrow! And you also know you need to know your credit score before obtaining a loan.

These are already two things you are going to do right!

To put yourself in the best possible position, here are some mistakes to avoid when trying to get a loan for your dream RV:

- **Not Shopping Around**: when you are researching loans, use the same strategy that I recommended for finding your dream motorhome. First get informed about your options, and only then pick the one that is most favorable for your situation. Visit a couple of banks, do your online research. Perhaps you already have an outstanding loan, and you can bundle it with a second loan at a discount, if you stick with the same provider?

- **Getting a Higher Loan Than You Can Afford**: before you get a loan, calculate what your income and expenses are going to be. You do not want to default on your loan payments, as this may trigger a clause in your contract that will increase your interest. When calculating your budget, do not only take day-to-day expenses like gas and groceries into account. Also factor in costs for maintenance, insurance, etc. When you are done, you may be surprised to see how little money is left that can be used to pay off the loan.

- **Getting a Loan That Exceeds the Future Sale Price of Your RV**: as we just covered, new RVs depreciate in value as much as 30% as soon as you take it around for its first spin. Never take out a loan for more than the future sale price. It would be best to make a big down payment when you buy the RV. And consider starting small. By buying a small RV, and selling or trading it in later on, you may be able to move your way up the RV ladder at a relatively low risk.

***

Preparing to purchase an RV, whether new or used, is an experience that requires preparation as well as patience. And how you are going to finance such a purchase is one of the most important things you will need to figure out. By applying the advice above, and doing your own research, you will have a solid foundation for finding the best possible way to finance your future motorhome.

Once the preparation, testing, and inspections have eventually led to the purchase of your beautiful recreational vehicle, it is time to prepare for your new living situation. Let's look into that now!

5. Preparing For RV Living

"There are no secrets to success. It is the result of preparation, hard work, and learning from failure."

Colin Powell

<u>Key Takeaway</u>: *The biggest obstacle you will tackle when preparing for RV living is choosing a state to domicile in. After that, everything else falls into place. Since you no longer have a physical address, go digital as much as possible. If necessary, use the address of your current campsite or local post office to receive regular mail or packages. You may need to find a workaround when it comes to voting, medical care, and jury duty. Use common sense here, and take it one step at a time. Keep in mind that these are small challenges when seen in the bigger perspective of living a life on the road!*

Getting ready for living in an RV full-time means setting a lot of moving parts in motion. Arranging things like voting, mail, bills, and taxes are usually filled with many different questions with no coherent source to find all of this knowledge.

We are here to change that.

***

Choosing a Domicile State

The very first step is deciding where you want to be from. When living a nomadic lifestyle such as this, picking a domicile state is essential. Once you have a legal permanent address, everything falls into place fairly easily. The great thing about living this type of lifestyle is the fact that you can actually choose which state to "reside" in. For one, this greatly impacts your taxes. But, being a resident somewhere and being domiciled are two different things: a residence means you are physically living in a specific location, but having a domicile means you live within a state's locality and have intent to take up residency there.

"Bodily presence" is a term thrown around quite a bit in state laws, and every state defines this term differently. But, one thing to take into consideration is whether or not you are earning an income. If you are, then states that do not have state income tax are usually most appealing. However, we will make this easy: of the states that do not have state income tax, South Dakota, Texas, and Florida are the most popular choices for people living a nomadic lifestyle because of the lack of state income tax as well as their overly-flexible definition of "resident."

However, there are other things to take into consideration when choosing a state to domicile in:

- Insurance rates
- Sales tax rates
- Vehicle registration fees and requirements
- Taxation on retirement proceeds and non-earned income (which is very important if you are living this sort of lifestyle off a 401-k, pension, Social Security, etc.)
- Property taxes

- Homeschooling laws (if you are living this lifestyle with children)
- And even the time that is required of you to live within the state

Where you wish to concentrate your state of domicile will depend on which of the above influences your lifestyle the most. But, two more important factors to consider when choosing a state of domicile are (i) your driver's license and tag renewal requirements – like whether you have to do it in person or not –, and (ii) jury duty obligations.

Yes, it can be a complex decision with researching and picking a state of domicile, but once you do, everything else easily falls into place.

The key to establishing intent for domicile is using that same address for everything:

- Insurance
- Vehicle registration
- Identification

- Taxes
  Voting
- Bank and credit card statements
- Bills, and
- Anything else that requires an address

The more "intent" you establish, the more rock-hard your "intent to settle" is, should it ever be called into question. Doing this allows you to cut ties with any other state you – or anyone else you live with – might have ties to, further proving your intent to settle.

However, establishing domicile status in a state does have its limits. If your nomadic life is going to come with living long enough in one state to establish residency anyway, then go ahead and make that your state of domicile. The reason why is that if your residency is ever called into question, and you are in a state that is more aggressive with taxes, they could potentially slap you with intent to evade statewide taxes as well as other fines that come with not registering your vehicle in a state you "obviously reside in."

***

How to Get a Permanent Address

Once you pick a state of domicile, it is time to get a permanent address. No, you cannot use a P.O. box as your primary address. One of the tactics is using a family member or friend's physical address. If you take this route, however, make sure it is someone you trust who is looking out for all of those important documents, such as:

- Jury summons
- Legal documents, and
- Tax notifications

Then, you need to set up with them how you will pick up that mail from them regularly (will they be holding it, trashing it, forwarding it to you somehow?). Another thing to consider is how stable their housing situation is. Why? Because if they move, you move.

However, in many states that are popular for nomadic travelers establishing domiciles, they have services that are specifically set up to support these types of issues. This service "gives" you a "permanent address" that can be legally used on everything:

- Bills
- Banking
- Voting
- Insurance
- IDs
- And everything else that needs proof of address.

Many of these services can also accept packages on your behalf and hold it for you, and some will even scan your mail electronically and forward it to you as they obtain it. There are fees with these services, but most of them charge under $10 a month for a basic package. Establishing one is very easy, with the process being only a simple sign-and-notarize process for some forms, and some power of attorney sheets if you want them to handle your vehicle registrations as well.

A point of warning, however: there are requirements by the Patriot Act to have an actual residential address on file for these types of accounts. This means that mail forwarding from a P.O. box or another service like this in another state is not acceptable. You are legally allowed to use a "next of kin" address in a different state, but do not try to explain your situation. This could call into question your domicile state, which then requires a whole lot of proof in terms of the residency of your forwarding address as well as your domicile intent in the state you have established.

***

Set up Electronic Deliveries

Once you have a state of domicile and a legal address to use, the easiest way to go about doing bills is going to be to convert them all to electronic deliveries. This will reduce the amount of overall mail you will have to be responsible for picking up, and it will make paying them easier. Why? Because online statements come with online links to pay online. Then, unsubscribe from all of those paper mailing lists and see if they have electronic ones. Just understand that snail mail is going to take some time before it catches up to your transitioning, and you will accumulate mail for a little while.

But, keeping track of things that will always come in the mail is necessary: know when your renewals for insurance policies happen and schedule a trip to get your mail. Know when your renewal tags will show up in the mail and prepare a trip to obtain them. Be proactive in these specific dates and times and get them down on a calendar that can easily remind you of the date, whether it is a hanging calendar or one on your phone.

***

Set up a Digital Signature

Many things, such as setting up voting and insurance, requires documents to be signed. But, it is not always practical to show up in person. Therefore, having a program that enables the electronic signature of documents is very important. Many official documents accept a digital signature, which means you could potentially eliminate paper mail even further than you already have at this point. This also comes in handy with contracts, selling big ticket items (such as cars), and handling insurance matters and issues.

For those that absolutely need to be filled out by hand, have a printer ready. These may be found at the campsite or post office, and if not, find a print shop in a town close by. Then, it is simply a matter of using an application on your phone, such as CamScanner, to take a picture of the document, scan it, enhance it, and shoot it back to the desired recipient via email.

***

Use the Campsite Address

There will still be times where you need a physical address to receive regular mail. Like when you order a package from Amazon.

Besides depending on local friends and family to receive your mail for you, another way to receive mail while being on the road legitimately is to use your current location at a campsite. Many campgrounds are happy to let you use their address for your mail, so long as you make your name and unit number on the campground clear to the person sending you the mail in the first place. There are some campgrounds that even service packaged deliveries to mailboxes that have the unit numbers on the grounds attached to them. Utilize the service if it is available!

***

Use the Local Post Office Address

One more way to receive mail or packages in a town you are residing in for a while is with general delivery. Basically, you can send your mail and packages to the town post office without having a P.O. box, and you can then pick it up as they are holding it behind the counter. They will hold all mail and packages up to 30 days, and it only takes your photo ID to claim everything.

A little trick? When ordering packages online, there is a way to have them delivered via general delivery: when you are filling out the shipping information and entering your billing address, click the button that says the delivery address is different from the billing one, then enter "PO BOX General Delivery" in the main address box. This forces many online retailers to default to a USPS delivery to the city and zip code specified.

***

Voting

In regards to voting, your legal domicile address is now what is used when you register to vote. Then, since you probably won't be showing up in person, make arrangements to have an absentee ballot sent out to you within plenty of time before the election date so you can fill it out and get it back in. It's as simple as that!

***

Medical Care

In terms of doctor's appointments and medical care, many cities have free clinics and medical centers that operate on a sliding scale, and some of these places simply provide the care at no cost to you. If your health insurance does not cover urgent cares and things of the sort in the state you are visiting, take advantage of these services.

Then, in terms of keeping your health records up to date, simply ask the doctor for an official copy of everything that was done. You can keep your own up to date healthcare records this way. The key to medical records is to keep them organized and readily available, whether you keep paper copies or electronic ones.

However, if you are over the age of 65 and on Medicare, then never fear: Medicare offers you benefits wherever you go, unless you are traveling outside of the U.S. If you are, purchase traveler's health insurance coverage to give you coverage just for these times.

Also, if you have past military service in your history and any service-related health conditions, you can acquire medical care via the Veterans Administration. While the coverage is determined by the length of time you served and your current annual income, it covers you anywhere you go as well.

If worrying about medications is an issue, then fret not: many medications with prescriptions can be ordered and delivered in the mail in 90-day supplies, and many pharmacies have nationwide servers so you can order your prescriptions from any pharmacy around the nation, so long as you use the same one.

***

Jury Duty

Another point of frustration for some full-time RV travelers is the civic duty of yourself as an American. Simply put: jury duty.

Some states are more forgiving of circumstances, and some are not. For those that are, simply explaining to them that you are out of town for a family outing suffices. For some courts, they will require you to reschedule once you are back in town, which makes this a hassle seeing as the point of traveling is to never be "back in town." For those types of courts, sometimes traveling back is the only way to go. This is something that needs to be worked into your savings budget: either a plane ticket back to your state of domicile to attend the jury duty gathering, or the gas money to take either the RV as a whole or the toad vehicle (the second vehicle many RV travelers haul behind their RVs), so the person being called into question for jury duty can make it back.

It is not a perfect plan, but attending jury duty in your state of domicile further cements your intent to settle, which will not bring your domicile status into question.

***

The hardest thing you will do, by far, is decide and establish your state of domicile. But once you do, many other moving parts fall into place simply by having a legal permanent address. There are downsides, like jury duty, that are sure to pop up along the way, but having a legal permanent address will help with many different billing and official matters in the long run.

But, this is not the only thing to reign in when choosing the nomadic life of living in an RV. The other big issue for you and your family is going to be your budget. How much do you need per month in order to be confident that you can pack your bags, toss them into the back of your new motorhome and hit the road?

6. How To Budget For The Road

"I've been flying down the road
And I've been starving to be alone
And independent from the scene that I've known"

Albuquerque – Neil Young

<u>Key Takeaway</u>: A budget is the biggest stressor for anyone on the road. Start with a budget of $1,000/month and assess whether this would be enough. It all depends on what is coming in and going out. If you can find ways to save money and cut costs, you will be able to lower your monthly budget. And that difference really adds up over the year. The most popular budgets still have full-time RV travelers working while on the road. If you are willing to stay in one location for a longer period of time, you could save up some money doing a seasonal job, working in a restaurant, or maybe even working at the campsite. An even better *solution would be to find a way to make money online, as this will truly make you location independent.*

So many people believe that a lavish fund of money is necessary to travel full-time and live this type of lifestyle. However, there are many people who travel and save for their necessities off simply $600 a month! Many of the tactics involved include putting back money and saving.

Many people who sit stationary in houses do not have the money to dole out of their checking account when car repairs are necessary. Usually, they pull that money from their savings account which they have been building for a few months.

The same concept applies when you are on the road.

***

Budget: Where to Start?

A good number to start with is a budget of $1,000 per month.

If you take the idea of $1,000 a month and break it down, a possible savings and split of money can look something like this:

- $50 in a savings account for vehicle maintenance and repair
- $200 for food
- $100 for vehicle insurance
- $50 for cell phone and internet access
- $250 for gas
- $25 for miscellaneous items
- $25 for entertainment, and

  $300 for on-road costs (such as nightly fees for campsites)

$50 in a savings account for vehicle maintenance and repair, $200 for food, $100 for vehicle insurance, $50 for cell phone and internet access, $250 for gas, $25 for miscellaneous items, and $25 for entertainment, and then $300 for on-road costs (such as nightly fees for campsites).

While the budget for food does not afford eating out every single night, it does afford you to eat well if you cook for yourself. The gas is also a bit low considering today's gas prices, but this simply means docking longer at campsites and possibly choosing campsites that allow you to dock for free in exchange for doing work around the campsite.

***

How to Save Money

Of course, there are many people who live off more than $1,000 a month while traveling, and then there are a lot who live off less. Those who live off less live a very sparse lifestyle, but the above rough outline shows you that the RV lifestyle can be done on as little as $1,000 a month. But, before any traveling scenario is taken on, making sure to have an accurate budget is necessary. And, if costs are an issue, there are always ways to cut them.

There are many different ways to save money. Here are some examples:

- Using smartphone apps that will be discussed later to chart out routes with the lowest gas prices
- Boondocking (parking overnight somewhere for free)
- Travel during off-peak driving hours so you do not waste gas sitting in traffic
- Regularly cleaning out the air filters in your RV
- Docking at campsites that offer free docking fees in exchange for voluntary work around the campsite, and
- Using surge protectors to keep your electronics safe

Many people who begin the lifestyle of living full-time in an RV can simply take the rent or mortgage money they were paying and transfer it over to the RV payment they now have. If you can purchase an RV with all cash, wonderful. However, many people cannot, so make sure the payment for the RV is worked into your monthly budget.

One way to offset some costs is to have a massive yard sale if you are choosing to live full-time out of your RV.

This can help you downsize a lot of unnecessary materials and make a little side cash in order to get you started on your first official trip.

A savings account is crucial for this type of lifestyle. An RV will require regular maintenance, and having that account will help to make sure your RV will be well taken care of, without throwing off your monthly budget when something eventually happens.

Many people simply take the money they were using on utility bills and begin putting that in their savings account. However, if you are looking to cut your cost of living, then take the amount of money you were using to pay bills, cut it in half, and put half of it back into that savings account.

When creating a budget, all areas of your lifestyle need to be taken into consideration:

- Groceries
- Gas
- Insurance

- Maintenance fees for your vehicle(s)
- Rent/mortgage, if you have another actual place of residence
- Subscription services (phone and internet are the big ones)
- Medical costs
- Prescriptions
- A regular deposit into a savings account
- Campsite fees, and
- Miscellaneous fees (entertainment, cleaning products, water softeners, clothes, feminine products, band-aids, etc.)

With regard to medical expenses, draw up an average of what your medical costs during the year look like, divide it by 12, and put that amount of money back into your savings account. This will help cushion medical issues that inevitably pop up with yourself and those you are residing with. If you have a pet, the same advice applies.

All of the above need a place in your budget. And remember, when in doubt, overestimate. It is better to have money left over then get on the road and not have enough.

***

Finding a Job on the Road

Another major question that comes into play is whether or not you will work on the road. Some people take up full-time residence in their RV later in life when their pension and Social Security are their forms of payment, and that is fine. However, others take up this lifestyle early on in life, and working on the road can become a confusing topic.

For some people, working seasonally gets them by. They spend their allotted money from their savings during the year, then stop somewhere nice for a season and pick up a job working for $7 or $8 an hour. They split their paychecks between their savings account and their daily needs until they have refueled their savings account back to where they need it to be for the coming months. Then they get back on the road once more and continue on with their journey. The key thing here is to keep up your resume and make sure to have solid references so you can continue to take on seasonal jobs.

Some people save costs simply by staying in one area for long periods of time. Many people stay in an area for three or four months at a time because they enjoy the culture or scenery, and while they are there they find a part-time job washing dishes in a restaurant or working part-time in a diner. This then provides them with money they need to sustain themselves while they are there without dipping into their savings account. They take the extra money they are not spending and put it back into their savings accounts to build it up for their next trek across the country.

If none of the above options are palatable to you in terms of making money on the road to facilitate the above basic budget breakdown, then there are many other options available to you to work while you travel:

- You can work at one of your campsites as a campground host, and some places offer free docking fees for those that do this type of thing

- You could make crafts and sell them places
- You could also offer handyman services or side-job construction type of work (such as painting)
- And you could even offer up services you were offering when you were dwelling in a home, such as animal grooming services or things like website design.

However, there are just as many ways to make money online as there are offline.

***

Finding an Online Source of Income

What would fit your new RV lifestyle even better is if you are able to find a way to make money online. More and more people are swapping their 9-to-5 job for a life as a so-called digital nomad. With digital devices becoming more sophisticated every year, and fast internet speeds being omnipresent across the country, NOW is an excellent time to learn how to make money online, so you can really become location independent.

I can only scratch the surface here, as an entire book could be written about every single way that you could make money online. With all these methods, keep in mind that none of these are a get-rich-quick scheme. Just because you are creating a business online does not mean it is easy. But if you would rather work hard typing away behind your computer than working hard doing a seasonal job in the fields, consider yourself lucky that you are living in the digital age. Just 15 years ago, you would not have the opportunity to choose between the two.

Here are some ways in which you can make money online.

***

Blogging

It is really easy these days to get your blog up and running quickly. You don't need to be a coding expert. Just pick a Wordpress template, or use an even more visual site like Squarespace.

If you are considering starting a blog to make money, you need to decide beforehand if you are willing to put in the necessary time to grow it. The most important thing with blogging is...blogging! You need to post regularly, at least once a week. Make sure you pick a niche and decide who your target audience is going to be. You cannot please everyone. Instead, pick a specific niche and really cater to your target audience. For example, the blog CheapRVLiving.com targets people that are into living the RV lifestyle on a budget. A great idea!

To make money of blogging you will first need to establish a reader base, and that takes time. In order to attract more readers, educate yourself on 'search engine optimization' (SEO) and use a plugin like Yoast to make your posts show up in Google for relevant keywords.

Include a few affiliate links in your posts, but always keep in mind that content is king. People have a very developed 'BS radar' these days. So if you are only blogging for money and do not really care about your content, you are probably going to shoot yourself in the foot. In that case, you may be better off choosing an alternative method to make money online.

***

Selling on Amazon

Amazon is the leading e-commerce store in the United States. It generated 136 billion U.S. dollars in 2016 net sales and has over 300 million active customer accounts worldwide. But did you know Amazon allows third parties to sell on their platform too? You could sell on Amazon!

The most popular format is called Fulfillment By Amazon, or FBA. Basically what this means is that, after you have sourced a private label product and sent the inventory to Amazon's warehouses, Amazon will fulfill a customer's order of your product. For a small fee, they take care of the payment, shipping and potential returns.

This requires an initial investment upfront, because you will need to buy inventory first. But once you have everything set up, and your product is selling, all you will need to do is making sure you don't run out of inventory! Because your products are stocked in Amazon's warehouses instead of in your garage, FBA is a great way of making money online while being on the road!

***

Drop shipping

Another way of selling physical products is drop shipping. There are similarities with Amazon FBA, but the main difference is that with drop shipping you are selling someone else's branded product, not your own. This will reduce your margins, so you will need to look into selling more expensive items. The flipside though is that you are not purchasing any inventory upfront. Instead, you find local wholesale suppliers and make yourself the middleman between them and the customer.

The process is basically as follows:

- Choose a profitable product to sell
- Contact suppliers
- Get approved by these suppliers
- Create a web shop (this can be your own website, an Amazon listing, or both)
- Drive traffic to it
- Start selling!

Selling products through Amazon's fulfillment system is becoming more and more popular, because Amazon is just such a huge e-commerce site. But drop shipping is still a viable alternative if you want to sell physical products.

***

Teaching English

There are many ways in which you can now teach English online to eager students all around the world. You can choose to start your own personal brand as an English teacher, and find students by giving away a ton of free value first. Think blog posts and Youtube videos.

But...you don't necessarily need to go out there and find your own students. Lots of online platforms are looking for native speakers to teach English to their students.

Here are some examples:

- Italki.com
- Verbalplanet.com
- iTutorGroup
- Nicetalk.com

Go check them out and see if teaching English online is something for you!

***

Freelancing

Do you have a specific skill set that you can monetize? Perhaps you are a good copywriter, or a graphic designer. Or maybe you speak multiple languages and can offer translation services? If so, this might be a great way of making some extra dollars on the road.

Even more so than with trying to land an online teaching job, there are a ton of websites that bring freelancers and potential clients together. Here are a few of the most popular websites:

- Upwork.com
- Fiverr.com
- Toptal.com
- Freelancer.com

There are also freelance websites that target specific niches, such as 99Designs.com for graphic design work. Do your own research and find the jobs that match your skills.

***

These are just a few ways in which you could make money online. And there are many more, such as creating video courses, starting a Youtube vlog, or affiliate marketing.

Whichever one you choose, do not spread yourself too thin. Understand that it takes time to build up traction for your blog or Amazon FBA product, or to build up a popular profile on Freelancing or English teaching websites.

Graham Bell once said: *"Concentrate all your thoughts upon the work at hand. The sun's rays do not burn until brought to a focus."*

Let this be your inspiration to focus on one thing. This will greatly increase your chances of knocking it out of the park!

7. Getting Along In An RV

"Sometimes I wonder how you put up with me. Then I remember, oh I put up with you, so we are even."

Popular Saying

Key Takeaway: *Just because you love and enjoy someone's company does not mean sharing an RV will always be fun and comfortable. Making sure everyone has their own space and responsibilities ensures peaceful traveling for everyone around the clock. Stick to your budget, communicate openly when things get heated, and you will get along great!*

Living in an RV full-time means residing in a much smaller space with those you care for. Whether it is your significant other or a pet, keeping the peace is just as much of a priority as saving money.

***

Make Sure Your RV Has Enough Room

The first thing to consider is whether or not the RV you are looking to purchase has enough room for everyone to live comfortably. If four people are attempting to maneuver in an RV cargo van, things are going to become miserable very quickly. This does not mean you have to go and spend hundreds of thousands of dollars on a massive bus, but it does mean that it is important that everyone has their own little space.

Remember: if you do not get along in a home, you will not get along in an RV!

***

Choose a Sturdy RV

Another thing to take into consideration is how sturdy the RV is. If traveling is the main goal for your decision to live in an RV full-time, then making sure it stands up to different weather changes is imperative. Being able to regulate the temperature well inside of the vehicle, no matter the conditions outside, will go a long way in making everyone comfortable.

***

Assign Roles

Make sure everyone has a role. For many, an RV needs at least a driver and a navigator. If the driver is attempting to do both, things become unsafe, but if someone is attempting to "backseat drive," things become tense.

Other roles in an RV are the "cleaner," who goes behind and makes sure things are latched for the road trip ahead and the "hunter," who makes sure none of the necessities are left behind (such as electronic chargers, outside chairs, etc.).

Dividing up the chores necessary every time you set up in a camp helps aid in getting space after traveling as well. If someone is responsible for the inward preparation, and someone else is responsible for the outward preparation, it creates automatic distance that can be exponentially important when traveling in a confined space with one another.

Respect Each Other's Storage Space

Yet another way to keep the peace is to respect each other's storage space. If one person begins to take over much of the storage space that is already limited within the RV, resentment can boil and arguments can happen. Divvy up the space accordingly and stick to it. It will help with things in the long run. One way to make sure no one overtakes any space is to not overpack. RV living is about downsizing. Knick knacks have no place (usually) and a massive and sprawling wardrobe will not work. If you are having trouble downsizing, then a monthly storage unit needs to be worked into your budget.

In an RV, everything has a place. Make sure to establish these places beforehand, and this will keep simple situations like "where is the boiling pot?" from escalating into intensely emotional situations.

***

Assign a Place For Your Pet

If you are traveling with pets, assigning them a place is imperative. The last thing you want is an animal darting in between your legs and underneath your feet as you are trying to maneuver (or drive) in an RV. Train them to sleep in that spot and be in that spot when the RV is moving. It will make a world of difference in how you live around your pet.

***

Avoid Clutter

Clutter is an RV's worst enemy and can lead to many arguments. Get into the habit of washing your dishes and storing them away whenever you are done eating. There are no barnyard sinks in RVs, so leaving dishes in the sink clutters a space very quickly. If you are someone who likes to toss their clothes around, then learn a new habit: put your clothes where they belong the moment they come off your body. An RV can seem much smaller very quickly once clutter begins to build.

***

Do Not Travel Too Much in One Day

Also, make sure not to travel too much in one day. RV living is about traveling, yes, but full-time RV living gives you all the time in the world to travel. This means traveling 10 hours in one day to go see that relative of yours is a thing of the past. Be leisurely. Take your time on the road. Never try to put more than 400 miles in a day on an RV. It will help you take in the scenery, as well as enjoy the traveling, rather than making that traveling a stressor.

***

Stick to Your Budget

A great way of making sure everyone gets along well is to prevent stressful situations.
One of the greatest tensions many experience when living on the road are the monetary fights.

That is why a whole chapter of this book is dedicated to calculating your budget! If you apply the lessons from that chapter, this stressor is eliminated from the high tensions already established with adjusting to living in a closer proximity to family and pets.

***

Communicate Openly

The most important way to keep the peace and diffuse highly emotional situations is to be communicative. Even if you are the type of person that needs space to breathe before tackling an emotional topic, you still need to be able to communicate clearly. Lack of communication between those dwelling in a small space like this will breed tensions and spawn raging arguments.

A book that may really help is 'The 5 Love Languages' by Gary Chapman. He argues that we can receive love in 5 different ways:

1. Acts of Service
2. Quality Time
3. Physical Touch
4. Receiving Gifts

5. Words of Affirmation

These are all love languages. Every person has a dominant love language. If that language is used when they are communicated with, they will feel loved the most. Now here is the key thing to take note of: Most partners do not share the same dominant love language!

And this is the cause of much friction. Because if we are not aware of the different love languages, we automatically project what works for us on our partner.

So your dominant love language may be 'Words of Affirmation', meaning you feel loved the most when your partner compliments you. But if your partner's dominant love language is 'Physical Touch', and you never hug her or hold her hand, there is going to be a problem: she is not going to feel loved. Even if you tell her "Honey you look stunning, I love you" 10 times per day!

If you are sharing an RV with others, you can really do a lot of damage control by learning about these love languages, and figuring out the preferred love language for you and your partner.

And if all else fails, lock yourself in the bathroom or take a walk to breathe, then emerge ready to talk.

***

There are many different ways to help establish peace in a full-time RV situation. Making sure you and your loved ones stay happy and on the same page means acknowledging, and accepting that everyone is different and needs their space and privacy. That space gives people a sense of independence and lays the groundwork for stress decompression on an individual level.

Luckily, there is one massive way to save money while on the road that can help eliminate budget stresses, and that has to do with where you stay overnight while on the road. It is called "boondocking," and it saves many travelers thousands of dollars over the course of an entire year.

8. Finding The Best Campgrounds, Paid Or Not

"The world is a book, and those who do not travel read only a page."

Saint Augustine

Key Takeaway: *The largest chunk of an RV budget, by far, are campgrounds and campsites. Boondocking is a way to save you thousands of dollars a year, but it is not for everyone. Even if you don't want to boondock, there are still ways to save on campsite fees.*

A main concern when living the RV lifestyle is where to park at night. Basically, you have two options:

- Boondocking
- A paid campsite

Paying a campsite needs no further explanation, but what is boondocking? We will look at that first, and then we will go over how you can use apps and various memberships to find a safe place to rest your head at night.

***

What is Boondocking

Boondocking is the phenomenon of utilizing nature itself, or a sanctioned parking lot, to dock for the night instead of paying a campsite. This has gone a long way in saving many individuals money because most of these places allow you to dock for free. The truth of the matter is that it is not always feasible to drive through the night (nor is it safe), and parking constantly at campgrounds can rack up a very serious bill. Therefore, many areas around the country, from free public lands to Walmart parking lots, all encourage the overnight docking of RVs.

But, how do you keep power? And water? Well, many people nowadays who live in an RV full-time are taking advantage of the tax credit that comes with installing solar panels and putting a few in specific areas of their RV. This gives them power no matter where they go and makes boondocking a lot easier. If you do not want to go full-on solar panel just yet, there are many portable solar panels that can be easily stored away when not necessary. However, you also have to keep that electricity usage efficient. Some ways to do that are not boondocking in areas that will require a constant use of the air conditioning or a heater, and switching the traditional bulbs in your RV to LED bulbs. Those will help save a lot of electricity in the long run.

With water, it is as simple as putting water into the outside reserve tank and using it. You know, like the water you use when you are traveling on the road. But, there is also the idea of water conservation. In order to boondock in luxury without having to worry about constantly refilling the water tank, there are things you can install and do to limit your overall water usage: install a low-flow shower head and a turn-off valve so you can shut the water off while you are lathering up. Low-flow faucet heads on your sink are also available, and if you want to invest in a solar shower (a small device that uses the sun streaming through your windows to heat up water in an insulated bag) for washing dishes and cleaning up, that will help conserve water as well.

But, how do you dump black water? And how do you know what areas will allow you to dock overnight for free?

Luckily, this is where smartphone apps come in handy.

***

Apps for Boondocking

You are very fortunate to live in today's world. Technology has advanced at an enormous speed these last decades. Did you know that by simply opening your browser on your smartphone you now have access to more information than Bill Clinton had when he was president?

Take a moment to let that sink in...

This is an amazing time to start considering living in an RV motorhome. There are so many online tools and apps at your disposal that I don't even know where to begin!

GasBuddy is a high-rated app that allows you to scour the nation for the lowest gas prices around. It works very well when planning your trips and trying to figure out how much gas will cost as you jump from state to state.

Some apps that will help you find boondocking stations are **US Public Lands** and the **Overnight Parking Walmart** app. Both of these will help you find free places to boondock for the evening to help plan your trip accordingly, and they will even provide addresses and phone numbers for people you can contact ahead of time if you have questions!

Yet another place that is friendly towards RV boondockers are truck stops, and there is an app called the **Truck Stops & Travel Plazas** that helps find truck stops that cater to RVs around the country.

However, the most useful app for people living in an RV full-time that boondock regularly to save money is the **RV Dumps** app. This is a sanitary dump locator for when your waste tanks are full and need to be dumped. It lists places with addresses all across the country, and also helps in planning trips. You can lay out a boondocking area that is near a dump, making everything seamless and worry-free for the road trip ahead.

One last app that many RVers use is **GPS Coordinates Finder**. Sometimes simply having your GPS coordinates can help whenever you get lost. And that is all this app does!

***

Campground Sites Memberships

If boondocking is not your thing, there are still ways to save money and have memberships at campground sites around the country.

For example, the **Good Sam RV Club** has a massive community that provides multiple services. They have a trip planning service that helps estimate fuel costs, aids in route planning, helps to locate other RV services (such as maintenancing) around your specific area, and helps locate viable rest stops along your route. Not only that, it provides a 10% discount upfront to any of their 1,600 camping sites in the U.S. and Canada.

But, their membership also includes things like emergency towing services, and can provide full RV coverage insurance for when you are traveling. It can help plug the holes in the insurance you already have, reducing your liability even more and keeping you worry-free throughout your journey.

Another club to join that can help reduce the costs of RV living is the **RV Golf Club**. The membership is $99/year, and this enables someone to park at several private golf courses and resorts for free. The locations have stunning views, no parking fee whatsoever, and this membership will help with discounts at the resorts and golf clubs if you are a golfer.

Harvest Hosts is a membership similar to RV Golf club, except it allows you to stay at parks of many listed wineries and specialty farms for free. Discounts on some of their products are available to those that have this membership, the docking is free, and the membership is only $40/year. The program currently has 470 sites, and it keeps on growing daily.

Escapees is another top-rated club, but it is more expensive than the others mentioned above. The membership fee is $39.95/year, and there is no enrollment fee. But, it does have other fees that rack up. This program offers shared discounts with other RV organizations that help save money on the road in the long run. It comes with benefits like 50% off at over 1,000 campgrounds across the nation, and the club itself has 19 five-star RV campgrounds where members can hook themselves up for $10-$15 dollars a night. The weekly rate for staying at a place like this is less than $100, which is beyond reasonable for long term stays, and those who want to dry camp (using their campsite without hooking up to their water and electricity) can park there for merely $5/night for up to 21 days!

***

It is very possible to keep campground sites and overnight fees from eating holes in your budget. These tactics alone can free up thousands of dollars a year, and can sometimes mean the difference between full-time RV living with a job versus without one. The above listed memberships are not the only ones available, but they are currently the top-rated ones in the nation. However, if boondocking is something you would want to do for simple overnight stays, then that is the biggest money-saver for many RV travelers.

Finding great campgrounds, no matter what you choose to do, is easy with the invention of tailored apps for smartphones. Use every single one of them to your benefit and you are sure to save a lot of money while you are traveling, while docking and camping in some of the nation's most beautiful terrain. Take advantage of the tax credits available to you to make boondocking a little more luxurious, and boondock offsite in public lands. Allow yourself to wake up to the sun rising over a sprawling lake as fish jump and thousands of birds serenade you in the background.

The views alone are priceless.

9. RV Resources

If you would like to learn more about RV Living, here are some great free resources to get you started.

***

RV Lifestyle Websites

- **Rvia.org**: Website of the Recreational Vehicle Industry Association (RVIA). Check out their calendar to find an RV show near you. Most shows are organized in spring, summer and fall.
- **CheapRVLiving.com**: Learn about how to live the RV lifestyle on the cheap.
- **TheRVGeeks.com**: Dedicated to educating you on RV maintenance, repair & travel tips. Also has an excellent Youtube channel with lots of educational videos.
- **Rvtravel.com**: Lots of info and advice for RVers here. Don't forget to subscribe to their great newsletter.

- **Technomadia.com**: Chris Dunphy, Cherie Ve Ard and their cat Kiki combine their expertise of technology with life on the road. Very inspirational if you are considering working online as a way to make money while traveling!
- **Doityourselfrv.com**: Great RV website, especially for those that consider themselves a DIY-expert.

***

RV Lifestyle Apps

- **GasBuddy**: Allows you to scour the nation for the lowest gas prices around.
- **US Public Lands**: Will help you find boondocking stations.
- **Overnight Parking Walmart**: Find Walmart locations where you are allowed to park your RV overnight.
- **Truck Stops & Travel Plazas**: Helps you find truck stops that cater to RVs.
- **RV Dumps**: Helps you locate places where you can dump the waste that has accumulated in your RV's waste tanks.

- **GPS Coordinates Finder**: Find your exact GPS coordinates. A lifesaver when you get lost!
- **Passport America**: Browse an international directory of 1900+ participating parks, campgrounds, and resorts.
- **CamScanner**: Take a photo of a document and make it look as if it was scanned. Perfect for when you need to submit a signed document.

***

Finding Campsites Websites

- **Roadnotes.com/product/walmart-rv-parking-directory/**: It is Walmart's official policy to allow RVers to park overnight on their parking lots. However, overnight parking is prohibited at approximately 800 Walmart stores (20% of all stores), mostly because of local laws and parking space availability. This PDF contains a list of all Walmart stores where it is not allowed to park your RV at night. Is your local Walmart not in the list? Then you are good to go!

- **Campendium.com**: Database of over 21,000 different campgrounds, many of which are reviewed by other users. Also has a database of sanitary dump stations.
- **FreeCampsites.net**: A community-driven platform for sharing campgrounds and campsites. Great place to find free camping sites near you
- **Boondockerswelcome.com**: Connect with other RVers to hear tips and tricks about boondocking and life on the road on a budget.
- **Passportamerica.com**: Offers a 50% discount at their participating 1,900+ campgrounds in the U.S.

***

Making Money Online Websites

- **Wordpress.org**: Build your own website.
- **Squarespace.com**: Another platform to build your own website, more visual than Wordpress.
- **Amazon.com/fba**: Sell Private Label products on Amazon through Fulfillment By Amazon.
- **Italki.com**: Teach English online.

- **Verbalplanet.com**: Teach English online.
- **iTutorGroup**: Teach English online.
- **Nicetalk.com**: Teach English online.
- **Upwork.com**: Find work as a freelancer.
- **Fiverr.com**: Find work as a freelancer.
- **Toptal.com**: Find work as a freelancer.
- **Freelancer.com**: Find work as a freelancer.

***

Membership Websites

- **GoodSamClub.com**: Massive community that provides multiple services, including trip planning and emergency towing service.
- **RVGolfClub.com**: Enables you to park at several private golf courses and resorts for free.
- **HarvestHosts.com**: Similar to RV Golf club, except it allows you to stay at parks of many listed wineries and specialty farms for free.
- **Escapees.com**: Another top-rated club. Offers shared discounts with other RV organizations that help save money on the road in the long run.

***

Roadside Assistance Websites

- Goodsamroadside.com
- Coach-Net.com
- Progressive.com

Conclusion

Thank you so much for taking the time to download this book *'RV Living: A Beginner's Guide To Turning Your Motorhome Dream Into Reality'*.

Now that you have read through it and digested the information at hand, you should have a thorough understanding of the basics that go into full-time RV living, how to create your own budget, how to choose which RV is right for you, and how to cope with the new lifestyle at hand. There are many moving parts that need to be jostled and changed when someone goes from living a stationary lifestyle to living a nomadic lifestyle, but that does not mean it cannot be navigated.

The key is research. Take it one step at a time and make sure you plan this out accordingly. Give yourself time to adjust as well as time to put everything together, and understand that everything comes with a learning curve.

Living in a recreational vehicle full-time can bring a fullness to life that stationary living sometimes cannot provide. For those wanting to live on a lower budget than they do now, RV living can provide exactly that. Enrich your life and travel. See the world around you. Meet new types of people and indulge in activities you never would have otherwise. That dream is possible with RV living.

I hope you have learned a lot about RV living, and feel comfortable – and excited – to make your dream of living in a motorhome come true!

***

BOOK 2 – SHIPPING CONTAINER HOMES: Learn How To Build Your Own Shipping Container House and Live Your Dream!

Introduction

Thank you for taking the time to purchase this book, *'Shipping Container Homes: Learn How To Build Your Own Shipping Container House and Live Your Dream!'* Clearly you have an interest in understanding what truly goes into building and living in your own shipping container home.

And you have come to the *right* place!

Over the last years, shipping container homes have grabbed the interest of:

- potential homeowners looking to enter the housing market for the first time
- retirees looking to spend their golden years in a domestic paradise, and
- successful professionals who want to fully own a home so they no longer have to slave away at a job they don't like just to pay their monthly mortgage payments.

Why? Because you get incredible value for your buck! With housing prices going through the roof, a shipping container home can be built for a fraction of the cost of a regular home.

Moreover, many shipping container homes are eco-friendly, resistant to extreme weather conditions and offer a high level of safety.

This book covers all facets of shipping container homes. It contains step-by-step instructions on how you can go about designing and building your own shipping container home, as well as guidelines in your selection.

At the completion of this book you will have a good understanding of what building a shipping container home entails, as well as what its main benefits and features are. So you can make an informed decision on whether this is the right choice for you.

If living in a shipping container home is your dream, **<u>now</u> is the day** on which you can take the **first step** to **changing your life**.

Thank you again for purchasing this book. I hope it will inspire you to make that dream come true. Welcome to the family!

Chapter One: What Are Shipping Container Homes?

"We decided to build the home out of shipping containers because it uses less energy to re-purpose them than to recycle them (melt them down and remold the metal into something else). They are also really cool looking and add a fun industrial feel to the home. They are metal so we can use magnets all over the walls and they are almost indestructible. It's the first shipping container residence in our city… so we thought it would be cool to build the first one here in my hometown!"

Ryan Naylor, on why he decided to build a home out of shipping containers.

<u>**Key Takeaway**</u>: *Shipping containers are sturdy, durable containers that are used to transport goods by*

sea all over the globe. Many of these shipping containers are only used once, and as a result can be bought for a low price. This, combined with the eco-friendly aspect of it, has sparked the trend of shipping container homes: converting these big steel containers into living spaces. Shipping containers have been used to build living accommodations for students and even shopping malls. In this book you will learn how you can go about designing and building your own shipping container home.

Purchasing or building a home is one of the biggest decisions you will make in your life, and possibly one of the most financially-taxing as well. There are many considerations you will need to put into account when selecting the type of house, how much space is necessary, design, materials, location, and other variables. It is a decision that has both short-term and long-term repercussions on your lifestyle, so you should equip yourself with as much knowledge and available options as possible.

In recent years, a trend that has grown in popularity among many home-buyers is the conversion of shipping containers into usable living spaces. How does that work?

***

Turning a Shipping Container Into a Home

Shipping containers are designed to carry all sorts of cargo by sea, to every corner of the world. They are made of steel, which makes them very sturdy. Also, they can withstand various elements of nature.

The majority of shipping containers in the world today come from China. It is estimated that there are around seventeen million of these containers around the world today.

Now check this: Many containers are only used once!

Did you know that? It blew my mind when I first heard it.

Often it is cheaper to let these one-trip containers gather dust at a shipping container graveyards close to shipping ports, than sending them back to their point of origin.

This, together with it being a cost-effective alternative to traditional housing options, has sparked the trend of converting these shipping containers into homes.

**

How Shipping Containers Are Used For Retail and Housing

Enterprising individuals have successfully converted these big steel containers into office or retail spaces worldwide.

For instance, in Le Havre, France, shipping containers were converted into 'Cité A Docks', a 100-apartment complex for students. Each unit is equipped with a bathroom, kitchen, and Wi-Fi access.

Cité A Docks, Le Havre

Something similar has been done in Amsterdam, The Netherlands. A lot of students struggle to find an apartment for a rent they can afford. To accommodate these students, the local government started the 'Keetwonen' project and had an impressive number of shipping container homes built. As a matter of fact, with 1,000 homes it is the world's largest container campus for students.

Keetwonen Project, Amsterdam

Meanwhile, in the United States, retailer Puma converted 24 shipping containers into a three-level, 11,000-square foot store and event venue. Dubbed as 'Puma City', the travelling store was completed in 2008 by the LOT-EK architectural firm, and has made stops in many cities.

Puma City

In a review of the Puma City concept store, Olivia Chen of Inhabit.com wrote: *"While the structure of the shipping containers is evident in the multiple frames created by the knocking down of the shipping containers' walls, the open and well-lit environment makes the industrial aesthetic seem almost intentional. Additionally, built-in details, such as the two decks located on the upper floors and recessed lighting, gives the store a greater sense a permanence and less like a prefabricated structure that can simply be folded up and moved."*

And finally, in Christchurch, New Zealand, a pop-up mall made from shipping containers was created after the 2011 earthquake in the city. Dubbed as 'Restart the Heart', the mall project made use of 60 shipping containers housing 27 shops.

Re:START mall, Christchurch

The Re:START mall project was initially envisioned to be a temporary retail space after the earthquake damaged much of the City Mall, but has become very popular among locals and tourists alike and it remains in business until today.

***

With the use of shipping containers becoming more and more mainstream for retail, office, and residences in many areas of the world, perhaps you are looking into this option as well.

Refurbishing shipping containers definitely offers a lot of flexibility and innovative design options for your home. Let's take a closer look at the advantages of converting these containers into residential units in the next chapter.

2. The Benefits of Shipping Container Homes

"They are structurally very strong and sturdy (easily stood up to category 5 cyclone Marcia and sustained no damage). They are also low cost and very environmentally friendly."

Stephan Busley, on the advantages of living in a shipping container home.

Key Takeaway: Shipping container homes are popular for a good reason: they have all the benefits of a traditional home, without any of the drawbacks. The most important benefits of shipping container homes are that they are cheap, sturdy and are widely available, can be ready for use quickly, and finally offer design creativity and flexibility.

What is it that draws so many people to wanting their own shipping container and build it into their home?

In this chapter we will cover the many advantages of choosing a container over a traditional home. So you can see for yourself if this is the type of you home you could see yourself living in!

***

Shipping Containers Are Cheap

Perhaps the most important benefit of considering a shipping container for your home is cost. Traditional homes are often very expensive, requiring you to take out a big mortgage loan with a hefty interest rate. If you can get a loan at all. Your credit score may be such that you do not qualify for a loan. And if you do, you may still not be able to purchase the house of your dreams because the amount of money you can borrow is limited, based on your annual salary.

Enter shipping containers.

Shipping container homes have all the benefits of traditional homes. But with one big difference: cost. A custom-built home made with one or more shipping containers, based on your specific wants and needs, can be obtained for as little as $30,000 - 40,000. That is not the price of the container, but the entire cost for building it into a home. The actual shipping container will cost much less, but you will also need to factor in other aspects such as creating the entire structure, designing the interior and decorating it. Still, this is a bargain compared to traditional homes.

Think of how living in a shipping container home will positively affect your monthly budget! Instead of paying a large sum in interest on a mortgage loan, you can now pay off your mortgage pretty quickly. And then be debt-free. Or, alternatively, reduce your monthly expenses simply by paying off less per month. Imagine the possibilities that come with freeing up these financial resources!

***

Shipping Containers are Sturdy

The purpose of shipping containers is to protect cargo that is transported by sea. These containers need to be able to withstand any meteorological conditions you can think of:

- Hurricanes
- Waves
- Winds
- Snow blizzards, and
- Storms

But also one you may not have thought of immediately: the glare of the direct sun.

That is why many shipping containers are made from weathering steel, also referred to as Corten steel. This is a group of steel alloys that resists the corrosive effects of rain, fog and other natural weather conditions by forming a coating of rust-like oxidation over the metal. This type of steel is also used to build bridges, which then hardly need any maintenance after construction is completed.

Because of these qualities, shipping container homes are actually much safer than traditional homes.

***

Shipping Containers are Widely Available

Let's look at another very obvious advantage of shipping container homes: their availability.

This would be especially convenient for people who live in port cities or in areas with large shipping industries, as these are typically where international freight ships would dock and unload their shipping containers. If you reside in an area with a large port used for international trade, you will likely be able to ask around and find shipping containers that are no longer in use and are available for reuse.

Many ports are struggling with the problem of where to store unused shipping containers from all over the world. In many cases, sending empty shipping containers back to their point of origin can be quite expensive, so many of these steel structures just sit in large storage areas.

Because there is such an oversupply of shipping containers, it is definitely a buyer's market. Many dealers are all too willing to sell them to people looking to repurpose the containers rather than deal with the upkeep of keeping them on-site. So drive a hard bargain!

Stacked shipping containers

***

Shipping Containers are Eco-Friendly

The massive oversupply of shipping containers in ports all around the world has inspired many environmentalists to drum up interest in repurposing these containers. Because returning them to their port of origin is often too costly, it makes a lot of sense – both economically and environmentally – to repurpose these containers by turning them into homes.
You are also limiting your carbon footprint by choosing a container as a home, because it already provides its own structure: it comes with its own walls and roof.

Keep in mind though that this benefit only applies to used shipping containers. If you order a brand new container, one that has never been used, it will roll straight out of the factory for you. Compare it to picking up a dog from a shelter versus getting a puppy from a breeder. Of course, puppies are super sweet! But choosing one over a shelter dog will not decrease the number of dogs staying in the dog shelter.

As a matter of fact, some even go as far as to be skeptical about the environmental benefits of shipping container homes. In a 2011 article, Brian Pagnotta of ArchDaily.com – which prides itself in being the world's most visited architecture website – noted that after all the modifications, not to mention the expense needed to transport the container, the ecological footprint could be just as big:

"Reusing containers seems to be a low energy alternative, however, few people factor in the amount of energy required to make the box habitable. The entire structure needs to be sandblasted bare, floors need to be replaced, and openings need to be cut with a torch or fireman's saw. The average container eventually produces nearly a thousand pounds of hazardous waste before it can be used as a structure. All of this, coupled with the fossil fuels required to move the container into place with heavy machinery, contribute significantly to its ecological footprint."

Still, it cannot be denied that the reuse of these massive steel boxes would be a better alternative than having them sit and add to the world's refuse.

Keep this in mind if 'going green' is your main reason for considering a shipping container as your future home. Building and living in one can definitely be more eco-friendly than a traditional home, but it depends on how you go about it.

***

Shipping Containers Can Be Ready For Use Quickly

Another advantage of shipping container homes is the relative speed in which they can be ready for use. This is also why shipping container homes are becoming popular options for re-housing people affected by natural calamities and other disasters in some areas of the world. They can be refurbished and ready for habitation in as little as two months. If you are pressed for time or just looking to move out of your current residence as soon as possible, you may find this a viable solution.

***

Shipping Containers Offer Design Creativity and Flexibility

In many areas, especially in large cities or highly-urbanized regions, it can be challenging trying to find a house that fits your needs. Attempting to build one from the ground up with the exact design you have in mind could also be cost-prohibitive.

By contrast, shipping container homes offer a lot of design creativity and flexibility. The basic structure can be repurposed in any way you deem fit. There are lots of modifications that need to be done before the shipping container can be considered as a living space. And how they are done is entirely up to you!

Shipping container homes allow you to design spaces that really reflect your personality, preferences, and needs. You may need just one container, or several, in order to execute the plan you have in mind. But the flexibility can be fun and can offer you a lot more personal satisfaction than having to settle for what is readily available on the housing market.

So if you are really looking to put your innovative ideas and creative juices to use, a shipping container home could be just right for you.

***

So, is a shipping container home the right option for you? Aside from the benefits already discussed, the choice also hinges a lot on where you want to live, your immediate and long-term needs, and the space you are looking to create. If you live in a region where shipping containers in good condition are readily available and where traditional housing options may be too costly, this alternative may make more sense than in other circumstances.

A shipping container home offers a wide range of freedom to the artistically-inclined and the creative individual at a relatively low cost. If you are really looking to create a living space that reflects who you are and your interests, this could be very attractive for you. Consider the flexibility as well; they can be ready for use quickly, and if you need more space, you may be able to just add to your original design by adding another container, for example if your family grows.

Of course, you would need to consider the location and the general climate in which your shipping container home will be built. Shipping containers are designed to resist extreme weather conditions. Still, discuss it with your architect or building firm. They will be able to address any natural elements that your home will protect you from, such as wind, rain, snow, dust, and other weather disturbances, and also be able to provide you with solutions for making the container home safe and comfortable.

Before you go ahead and purchase a shipping container though, there are a few things you need to consider first.

3. What to Consider Before Purchasing a Shipping Container

"My advice would be to do as much research as possible before the start of the project. It's all about preparation. There isn't a silver bullet approach to research. I guess the more you know and learn about shipping container homes before you start making decisions will help you to fail less. But again, there isn't a silver bullet approach to this. Failures along the way are inevitable."

Marek Kuziel, owner of a shipping container home.

Key Takeaway: There are many benefits to converting a shipping container into a home. However, there are also some things you need to consider before going ahead. Old shipping containers could contain *toxic chemicals. Your best option would be to purchase a new or one-trip container. Furthermore, allocate some funds in your budget for proper insulation, as it can get scorching hot or arctic cold inside without it. Finally, read up on local building and safety regulations to save yourself from a lot of headaches later on.*

In 2016, the floating student residence Urban Rigger was delivered in Copenhagen, Denmark. This carbon neutral property is entirely made from shipping containers. It was created to provide sustainable, affordable homes for students in European cities that are costly to live in.

Urban Rigger, Copenhagen

The Urban Rigger has been nominated for the Danish Design Award 2017 and Edison Awards 2017. This is yet another example of the creative use of shipping containers in order to provide homes to people who cannot afford a traditional home.

We just covered the many benefits of shipping container homes. Are you starting to get excited? I hope you are a few steps closer now to realizing your dream of living in one, some day soon.

However, it is not all rainbows and butterflies. There are some things you need to consider before going ahead and purchasing a shipping container.

***

Used Shipping Containers Could Contain Toxic Chemicals

You do need to be aware of some potential risks to your health in the chemicals used for the construction of steel containers, among them chromate, phosphorus, and lead-based paints. These chemicals make the shipping container sturdy enough for transport across continents, but they can also be harmful to humans in extremely high levels, or under prolonged exposure.

Moreover, some of the goods that are carried in these containers may also contain harmful substances, or even be toxic. Prolonged or excessive exposure to these pesticides can pose risks to your health.

We will discuss these chemicals in more detail in chapter 3 *'Are Shipping Container Homes Safe?'*, as well as how to remove them.

For now, remember that it would be best to only buy a new or one-trip container. This minimizes the risk of exposure to unhealthy chemicals.

***

Budget for Insulation

Another thing to consider is the additional effort and cost it can take to insulate the shipping container for the weather conditions in your area.

Steel conducts heat very well. If you live in a warm climate without proper insulation, it can get scorching hot inside. Conversely, if you live in a cold climate without proper insulation it can get arctic cold in your home.

This is less of a concern in moderate climates. However, even for areas with relatively mild weather most of the year, you will still need to refurbish the steel container for heat and cold, both of which can be magnified within the steel space.

Keep this in mind when calculating the budget for building your shipping container home.

***

Educate Yourself on Local Building/ Safety Regulations

The shipping container home you eventually build will have to comply with building and safety regulations in your area. Unless the area is very remote, you will very likely need a building permit. The exact set of rules that you will need to comply with will vary, depending on where you plan to live.

We will cover this in more depth in chapter 8 *'Building Permit and Other Legal Requirements'*.

For now, research the relevant local regulations before you even purchase a shipping container. If you don't, and build your shipping container home without a permit or violating certain regulations, you may be ordered to undo all your hard work, take it down, and possibly even remove the container from your property altogether.

Spend some time, and perhaps a little bit of money for sound advice, now and save yourself a lot of trouble later.

***

After weighing the pros and cons of living in a shipping container home, you can make an informed and educated decision on whether this is the type of home you would like to live for the foreseeable future.

If you do, the next step is picking the *right* container *for you.* Let's take a look at the different types of containers and their cost in the next chapter.

4. Choosing the Right Shipping Container

"I wish I knew that there were containers that are taller than 8 foot."

Mark Wellen (Rhotenberry Wellen Architects), on designing the Cinco Camp retreat, which was created entirely with shipping containers.

Key Takeaway: *There is so much hype about just how affordable container homes can be compared to other housing options. But while you can expect to save lots of money with this option, you still need to plan ahead and know what expenditures to expect, whether it is DIY or prefabricated. Generally speaking, shipping containers are available in two types: regular and high cube. Both are available in a 20 feet and 40 feet variation. The price depends on type, size and whether the container is new or used. You will also need to* *factor in cost for transport, design, labor and materials. If you are willing to pay a little bit extra to avoid the hassle of doing everything yourself, an interesting alternative could be a prefabricated container home.*

The cost is one of the biggest considerations for most people when it comes to choosing the type of home they want to purchase, and rightfully so. Housing expenses are probably the biggest for any individual or family, and typically includes mortgage or rent, taxes, maintenance and upkeep, utilities, and other related expenditures. It is important to carefully weigh the cost of housing because there are also other financial investments you will need to allot money for.

Promoters of shipping container homes frequently tout their relative affordability and availability compared to other types of housing, including subdivisions, town homes, condominiums, apartments, and other options. In highly urbanized localities and major cities, housing costs continue to rise, and comfortable living spaces that fit your financial means can be difficult to find.

By converting a shipping container into a home, you can tackle that problem.

But what can you expect to pay for a shipping container? That depends not only on whether it is new or used, but also on the type of container.

***

Shipping Container Sizes

There are two types of shipping containers that can be acquired for repurposing into residential use:

- **Regular**, and
- **High Cube**

Regular size containers are available in two variations:

- **20 feet long**, with these dimensions: 20 feet (length) x 8 feet (width) x 8,6 feet (height); and

- **40 feet long**, with these dimensions: 40 feet (length) x 8 feet (width) x 8,6 feet (height)

High cube containers are available in the same two variations, with one difference: they are **1 feet taller**.

So there are two things you need to consider:

1. Which length do you prefer?
2. Which height do you prefer?

Length: the main thing you will need to decide on is the container's length. Any of the two standard sizes – 20 feet or 40 feet long – could be modified into small homes. Which one would work best for you depends on your preferences. A 20 feet long shipping container may be enough for one or possibly two people. A 40 feet long shipping container on the other hand provides more space, and is
definitely recommendable if you have a family.

Keep in mind that you are not limited by the size of one container. If you need more space, you can purchase additional shipping containers to add to your home. These containers can even be stacked on top of each other to form multi-story houses, but with added cost.

A word of **caution** though: if you choose to weld multiple containers together, absolutely make sure that these containers were produced by the same manufacturer. Even though shipping containers come in just a few standard sizes, there are slight size variances which may only show once you are trying to stack and weld them together. Moreover, the size variance also makes insulation of your home more complicated.

Height: the other thing you will need to decide on is how tall your container home is going to be. The additional one feet in height that a high cube container offers may not seem like much when you are building your home, but once it is completed and you are living in it, the contrast with a regular container can be immense. And then it is too late to make any changes.

Compared to traditional homes, shipping container homes are tiny. At least, they can feel that way. If you are claustrophobic, you probably shouldn't even consider moving into a shipping container home. But also if you are comfortable in small spaces, an oppressively low ceiling can make you feel as if the walls are coming at you.

The container dimensions can also give you the wrong idea about the size of your actual living space: insulating the container will result in less room inside to move around.

There are a few downsides to high cube containers though, compared to regular containers:

- **They are more expensive:** Regular containers are more widely available, because these are the ones that are used the most in the shipping industry.
- **They are less eco-friendly:** Because it is rare to find one that has been used priorly to carry goods, you are probably only able to buy one straight from the factory. If you are inspired by the eco-friendly aspect of living in a shipping container homes, than high cube containers may not be your best option.

- **They are heavier:** Transport will be more costly, not only because of the weight difference, but also because some semi trucks are not equipped to carry such a heavy load.

Still, high cube containers are considered the best containers to convert into a home. So if these concerns are something you are willing to overlook, than I definitely suggest going for a high cube container.

***

What Does a Shipping Container Cost?

What you will have to pay for a shipping container depends on a number of factors, such as location, availability, size, and whether it is new or used. However, here are some ballpark figures of what you can expect to pay:

- **New 20-footer:** $2,000 - $5,000
- **Used 20-footer:** $1,750 - $4,500
- **New 40-footer:** $3,500 - $7,000
- **Used 40-footer:** $2,500 - $5,500

As you see, the range of these estimates is still pretty wide. The price for high cube containers will be on the higher end of the spectrum. Expect the price of regular shipping containers to be more in the low to mid-range.

This is only the price for the shell. If you just buy the shipping container, you will also need to budget for the costs necessary to convert it into a livable home. Even more so if you want to modify it to your own specifications.

***

Other Costs to Take Into Account

The first additional cost you need to account for is transportation: getting the shipping container from where it is docked or stored to your building location. Transportation costs will vary, depending on whether your container needs to be shipped to your area via land or sea. To reduce costs, start by looking for containers that are stored in shipping areas or ports close to where you live. Also, make sure that any price given to you for the shipping container itself already includes transportation and/or shipping costs. Remember that this is a buyer's market!

Another expense you need to factor in are labor and materials cost. If you have experience in construction or design and you are planning to do the necessary refurbishing and insulating yourself, this will greatly reduce the labor cost, which can range from $50 up to $150 per hour. But if you are hiring workmen for the job, expect higher costs.

If you already have a design in mind and just need a ready shipping container to implement your ideas, it may be best to look for an option somewhere in the middle, such as a shipping container that has already been cleaned, modified, and is ready for additional insulation, plumbing, and other interior and exterior details. Once you get the unit, you can then add whatever other enhancements you are able to do on your own, and save on the labor expense.

One alternative way which you may want to look into is getting designs and interior plans from artists or college students in your area. They may be looking for internships or other opportunities to enhance their skills as well as add to their portfolio. Shipping container homes are a popular trend these days, especially among younger, more environment-conscious individuals who are championing the cause of eco-friendly repurposing. This could be a win-win situation for both of you!

You may be able to contact college students or artists in your location that would be all too willing to use their talents and skills to help you design a creative, comfortable, and cost-effective living space. The cost of working with these up-and-coming designers, architects, and planners would certainly be less compared to what you would need to shell out for a large, established firm providing the same services. Of course, you do need to make sure that any plans or layouts given to you take note of structural integrity, occupant safety, building code regulations, and other important variables. But aspiring architects and designers are already aware of this and may be able to give you valuable insights without charging too much, as long as they can add your home project to their portfolio.

If you do decide to go with a professional firm for the refurbishing of your shipping container home, it would be more advisable to work with just one company that handles it all, from the cleaning to the finishing touches. This way, you can establish a clear theme and unified goal from the start, and also reduce or eliminate the possibility of mismatched or incompatible materials or designs in between the stages of the modification. Communication would also be easier if you are working with just one contractor that can handle the entire process.

As far as costs go, do not hesitate to pay more for superior quality for the most necessary details, especially when it comes to safety and comfort. Remember, you are the one who will be living in that space, presumably for a long time, after all the modifications have been completed. If the designer or engineer suggests a type of material or add-on for more protection against the elements, it is better to consider it rather than trying to cut expenses now and then paying for it later.

On the other hand, it is also true that more expensive does not always mean better quality. With the rise of DIY home building and improvement, you are sure to find cheaper ingredients and solutions that work just as well as others. The important thing to focus on is a home that you will be excited to live in, provides comfort and protection for you and your loved ones, and can be your place of refuge and rest.

***

Prefabricated Shipping Container Homes

Now, if this whole process seems a little bit daunting and you don't mind paying a little bit extra to take a shortcut, there is another option: prefabricated shipping container homes.

Increasingly, there are companies and design firms that have capitalized on the growing popularity of shipping container homes, and they are now selling ready-made shipping container homes to customers.

The prices for prefabricated shipping container homes can range from anywhere between $15,000 for the basic designs, and all the way up to $200,000 for larger or more sophisticated exteriors and interiors. Compared to home prices in most municipalities today, prefabricated shipping container homes certainly seem like a cost-effective alternative, and you may even find a manufacturer that can make additional modifications to your unit as needed.

Another upside to predesigned shipping container homes is that they are already fitted to comply with most local building codes and regulations. This means you will not have a very difficult time figuring out if the designs you want to put in place would be applicable for where you live. Manufacturers can also assist you with many other aspects of the construction and installation, including the right foundation, maintenance, and other modifications you may be interested in.

For many people with hectic schedules and not a lot of time to set aside for building or construction, purchasing prefabricated shipping container homes may just be the better option. You can look at different homes, pick out what you like, ask if there are modifications that can be added, and then the completed unit can be sent to you, ready for use.

***

Those are the basics you need in order to choose the shipping container that is right *for you*: type, size, price and costs.

What you will ultimately end up paying may be somewhat higher or lower than you originally anticipated, as it will ultimately depend on the details of the home and the effort required for the modification.

Purchasing a shipping container and hiring contractors will give you a lot of freedom to design your future home in any way you see fit.

On the other hand, by purchasing a prefabricated unit, you will save time and effort in picking out additional materials, interior plans, paint, and other sprucing up that would be needed if you just bought a new or used shipping container as is.

The choice is yours...

5. Are Shipping Container Homes Safe?

"It's definitely unsafe to use the old ones, they're really the unknown. I wouldn't touch them with a ten-foot pole. Used shipping containers can have high levels of chemical residue – they are coated in lead-based paint to withstand ocean spray."

Jamie van Tongeren (CEO of Container Build Group in Australia) on purchasing old shipping containers for residential use.

Key Takeaway: Like with any home, there are certain safety precautions you need to take. Used shipping containers are often coated with harmful chemicals, and their wooden floors treated with pesticides. Sandblast the container and take out the wooden floors, and you have nothing to worry about. To ensure your family's safety once you have moved *into your new shipping container home, make sure your container is built on a solid foundation, and fire extinguishers, proper locks and electrical wiring are all in place and function well.*

When considering your new home, it is a must to consider the safety of the location, structure, design, materials, and other components. After all, you will be spending a lot of time within the walls of your home, so it should be able to provide you with a secure and protected space for your personal activities. A home is an investment, so safety is one of the top priorities for any homemaker.

There has been much discussion about the safety and integrity of shipping containers repurposed as living spaces. We already briefly touched upon that earlier in this book. Because it is a fairly new concept, there are still many misconceptions regarding these residential units. If you are seriously considering whether shipping container homes are right for you, you must look into the facts and find out exactly what you are getting yourself into.

***

Used Shipping Containers Are Coated With Harmful Chemicals

If you have only seen shipping containers from afar, on television or in movies, then perhaps you do not have a clear understanding yet of just how sturdy these steel containers can be. Steel can withstand most any natural weather conditions you can think of – hurricanes, winds, blizzards, dust storms – so you have a building material that is known universally for its reliability and strength.

Remember that shipping containers were designed to hold cargo and transport all kinds of goods and produce to international ports, so safety and durability were of the utmost concern in their original design, especially because they would be out at sea for weeks, even months at a time. Shipping containers were constructed with storms and violent ocean weather conditions in mind.

One potential health hazard as far as shipping container homes go, however, are the chemicals that may be contained in a used shipping container. What you may not be aware of is that these containers are not just sturdy because they are made of steel, but also because they are coated with potentially harmful chemicals like chromate and phosphorous, in order to make them even sturdier. The walls may also be coated with lead-based paints.

Although brief exposure to these chemicals may be harmless, inhaling them on a daily basis in your living room is a totally different ball game.

***

Container Floors Are Treated With Pesticides

One of the most common cargo to transport is agricultural produce. The vegetables and other produce are placed on wooden floors in the container. These wooden floors are often treated with pesticides and other chemicals, in order to keep insects, fungi and pests away during transport.

A residue of these chemicals may still be found in the wooden floors of the used shipping container you are considering to purchase. These chemicals can be really dangerous! If not dealt with, they can cause respiratory difficulties, allergies and even organ damage when you keep them in your shipping container home.

***

What Can You Do To Remove These Chemicals?

Now that you are aware of the potential health hazards of shipping containers, what do you need to do to ensure your safety when you are moving and make it your home?

To start with, this is only a concern if you are buying a used shipping container. If you buy a new container, you can simply instruct the manufacturer that you are only interested in a shipping container that has not been coated with (potentially) hazardous chemicals, and does not have treated floors. And if you are going for a prefabricated unit, communicate with the manufacturer about safety precautions and procedures they have already undertaken to ensure that your unit is safe to live in.

With used containers, you need to be more careful. To mitigate any health risks posed by chemicals used in the shipping containers, it is always advisable to check with the manufacturer you are purchasing from and find out what the history of the container is. These containers are tracked using identification numbers and other tags, so it can be readily identified whether they were used for carrying agricultural produce, and if any pesticides or chemicals were utilized in the past.

If at all possible, check the shipping container you are purchasing personally before making any final decisions. This will give you a clear perspective of the quality of the container you will be getting, and the condition it is in.

Your best option is to sandblast the whole container. Sandblasting the entire container is absolutely a necessity, because it removes most – if not all – of the toxic coatings. If you then encapsulate the container in an enamel or polyurethane rust-resistant paint, your shipping container will be spick and span for many years to come.

With regard to treated wooden floors: do not be cheap here by deciding to keep them, thinking you will save some money by not replacing the floor. You will not: not taking these floors out can lead to high medical bills in the future. And by then, it is both your wallet *and* health that are suffering.

I strongly recommend to take out the wooden floors and replace them completely. Alternatively, use an encapsulation method where the dangerous vapors are firmly enclosed. If you go for the latter option, have an expert measure the air quality inside and confirm the container is safe to live in.

***

Laying a Solid Foundation

One of the most common discussions on the safety of shipping container homes is their ability to withstand violent climate conditions such as hurricanes, cyclones, or tornadoes.

Aside from the generally proven sturdiness of shipping containers, one other thing that you can do to protect your loved ones and yourself is making sure your shipping container home is built on a solid foundation.

There are roughly 4 different foundation types:

1. Full basement
2. Submerged crawl space
3. Flush crawl space, and
4. Slab-on-grade

Different construction methods can be used for every one of those foundation types, including:

- Concrete block
- Precast concrete
- Cast in place concrete, and
- Treated wood

Which foundation type is best for your shipping container depends on a number of factors, such as climate, site conditions, building design, and of course cost.

Consult with your designer and/or contractor to see which foundation type and construction method are best to use in your case. And check local regulations, to ensure you stay in line with your city's building safety codes.

***

Indoor Safety Precautions

Finally, common sense dictates that the most basic safety precautions in traditional homes should also be present in shipping container homes, such as:

- ☐ Fire extinguishers
- ☐ Locks
- ☐ Proper electrical wiring
- ☐ Alarm systems, and
- ☐ Other features

These safety features are all incorporated into the design and layout of a shipping container home, and for the most part these are just as common as what you would expect in a traditional home setting.

***

There are risks involved in just about any home selection you can think of. Some risks are man-made, while others are nature-related. Shipping container homes are no exception.

But you now know what you can expect, so you can face any challenges heads-on. Apply the safety precautions that we discussed, and don't forget to ask your contractors for advice. The safety of your loved ones and yourself should be your number 1 priority!

6. How To Design A Shipping Container Home

"I wish I knew how to insulate the shipping container, we ended up soldering elements on the walls and then sprayed them with a foam anti-fire insulation. Also I wanted to know how to keep the sun off the roof; in the end we did this by double ventilating the roof."

Arnold Aarssen (Studio ArTe) on what he wish he had known before building the Nomad Living Guesthouse in Portugal.

<u>Key Takeaway</u>: Building a container home from the ground up can be overwhelming, but definitely satisfying as well! Unless you are an experienced home designer or builder, you would do best to hire a pro to assist you in realizing your shipping container home dream. Do not use free floor plans you find online to build your container home. Although they can be *helpful in inspiring ideas, they are mostly clickbait. Instead, purchase a floor plan template or ask your architect to create a custom floor plan. Other things to consider are: floor selection, choosing the right foundation, proper temperature and noise insulation, using the right toolset, and adding a hip roof. You are in the driver's seat and will get to see your ideas come to life, so enjoy the ride but make sure all bases are covered. Plan ahead, and stay on track.*

Many people would go for the convenience and ready-made designs of prefabricated shipping container homes. After all, if manufacturers already have visually-appealing designs and are also able to make certain modifications to fit your needs and your lifestyle, purchasing ready-made shipping container homes would save you from a lot of the stress that comes with laying out your own home design, selecting building materials, hiring construction crews, and the other details involved.

However, for those who like the challenge of do-it-yourself building and designing, all of the tasks involved in building a shipping container home from the start would be welcome and enjoyable. This hands-on project really allows you to put your designing, engineering, and creative skills to the test!

A container house made with a single shipping container

If you have decided to do this on your own, the good news is you have a lot more control over the kind of home you will be living in, and the sky's the limit as far as the innovations and concepts you want to apply to your project.

So where do you start?

***

Hire a Pro

If you have decided on the size of the shipping container you will purchase, having an architectural layout of the home would be the next thing you need. If you have the architectural skills to draw out a plan, this is much better and will save you a lot of money. However, if you have a solid concept in mind yet lack the architectural or engineering skills to execute the plan, you would do well to consult with a professional.

As we touched on earlier, you may also want to consult with students in the fields of architecture or engineering who would be willing to assist you with the layout of the blueprint, and would command lower prices than professional firms. In exchange, you can allow them to use whatever plans or designs they come up with in their portfolio, and to also showcase their finished product as they look for work.

***

Choose the Right Foundation

In most localities around the world, the foundation of any building structure is part of the building codes and regulations, so after you have a layout or blueprint in hand, you will need to consider the type of foundation your home will require. Most shipping container homes are built with the traditional concrete block foundation, but you can also look into crawl space or basement-type foundations. Factors to consider when deciding the type of foundation your shipping container will need include soil type, bedrock type, weather conditions, and water tables, among others.

***

Floor Plans

With the vast amount of information you can find online regarding shipping container homes, you need not worry about where to get learning resources or ideas for each step of the planning and construction. In addition, you will find plenty of sample floor plans on the Web that can inspire your own final designs for your shipping container home.

These sample floor plans can be especially helpful if you do not have much experience with layouts or architectural drawings but have some ideas on how you would like the project to turn out. If you are going with a professional architect or engineer for the design, you can refer to a sample floor plan and let the professional know you are interested in something similar. They can then let you know if that is feasible for your situation.

A word of **caution** though: there is a difference between a home *design* and an actual *plan*! You can find all kinds of home designs online for free, but they cannot be used to actually build your shipping container home. Often, architects simply use these free designs as click-bait to get you to either purchase a template floor plan or hire them to design a custom plan for you.

According to the container homes association 'ISBU' – short for: Intermodal Steel Building Units and Container Homes – you can expect to pay approximately $1000 for a blueprint, $1800 for a PDF File and even $3500 for a CAD file. And those are prices for templates. Custom plans will be more expensive. So you can understand why that click-bait could be worthwhile...

Don't just print a random free design or plan that you found online and use that to build your shipping container home! You will regret it later.

With that said, here a few sample shipping container home floor plans and designs that can be found online (go to your web browser and type in the URL):

- **One bedroom, one bath, with a lounging deck**: bit.ly/sampleplan1

- ☐ **Two bedroom, one bath**: bit.ly/sampleplan2
- ☐ **Three bedroom, two bath**: bit.ly/sampleplan3
- ☐ **Three bedroom, two bath**: bit.ly/sampleplan4
- ☐ **15 different plans on a single page**: bit.ly/sampleplan5

Use them for inspiration only, and then either purchase a template or ask an architect to create a plan based on your instructions.

***

Floor Selection

As we discussed earlier, wooden floors in used shipping containers have most likely been treated with hazardous pesticides. Either take them out and replace them, or use other materials for covering up the floor, such as industrial epoxy or polyurethane coating. Do not do this without consulting an expert: you do not want to take any chances with your – or your family's – health.

Because of the steel frame of the container, it may not be a good idea to consider very thick carpeting for the interior of your shipping container home, as this can add to the heat during the warmer months. Lighter carpets and area rugs, however, are fine to use and can also add to the interior segmentation of your container home, as well as aid in soundproofing.

***

Plumbing Work

There is this urban legend that a container house cannot have a regular toilet, and you will need to install a freestanding composting toilet outside instead.

Nothing could be further from the truth.

You just need to decide *where* you want your toilet to be. Inside. Also lay out the plumbing work for your bathroom and kitchen, both incoming and outgoing water.

***

Electrical Wiring

Map out the electrical work: the location of switches and outlet points. For safety reasons, only use electrical outlets inside. Also, do not use regular switch boxes. Instead, use boxes that are thin enough to fit in the walls, and that do not conduct electricity in case of wiring mishaps.

Unless you are have experience with wiring, I recommend hiring a professional to help you install the wiring correctly.

***

Temperature and Noise Insulation

The next thing you will need to consider is insulation.

You are already aware that steel shipping containers can get very warm inside especially during the summer, so insulation would be your next factor to consider in the designing and planning stage of your container home.

What many don't realize is that cold temperatures can also be particularly magnified inside a shipping container home, so proper insulation is necessary whether your location has warmer or colder temperatures. Insulation for shipping container units can start with a closed-cell foam layer applied to the inner and outer walls of the entire structure. This simple layer of protection will keep out most problems with heat, cold, precipitation, and other elements.

If you live in an area with a warmer climate or particularly long, hot summer months, you would want to consider applying reflective paint on the outside of your shipping container home. Reflective paint bounces off much of the sun's rays and the heat, and can help in keeping the temperature inside cooler. Ceramic-based spray paints for the home interior can also help insulate versus hot temperatures while preventing the formation of mold, rust, or mildew. Many shipping container home designers also recommend SuperTherm.

Shipping containers can withstand up to 175 mile-per-hour winds, making them excellent housing options for areas that are prone to storms or hurricanes. However, hearing that howling wind and strong rains while you are inside can be quite a frightening experience. When you discuss insulation with your designer and contractor, do not limit those talks to temperature isolation. Soundproofing your shipping container from the noise outside is equally important.

***

Use the Right Toolset

With all the modifications you will need to do to the shipping container, particularly doors and windows, you will also need to figure out what tools you will require in order to cut through the steel of the container.

One tool you will need is a cutting disk, which may seem basic but will be very handy for your steel-cutting tasks. A word of **caution**: when using a cutting disk, there will be sparks and pieces of metal flying everywhere, so make sure you have protective gear on. The blades will also need to be replaced quite a few times.

Other cutting tools you may require include a:

- reciprocating saw, and a
- plasma cutter

A reciprocating saw, also called a sawzall, does not need to be replaced as often as the cutting disk (be sure to get one that is industrial strength).

A plasma cutter cuts through the metal by melting it with compressed air and electricity, and is the most efficient for cutting steel, although more expensive to maintain and replace. If you are looking for the quickest and best way to cut through the steel for windows, doors, and other modifications, a plasma cutter would be the best option, but it would also cost a bit more.

**

Consider a Hip Roof

When a shipping container is repurposed into a home, one of the many advantages is that it already comes with a very durable roof that is just as sturdy as the walls.

This makes your home quite the shelter during extreme weather events.

However, a shipping container was originally designed for storage, so if you are joining two or more containers to build a multi-storied structure, the roof design may be prone to water buildup and corrosion.

The solution to this would be to place a simple hip roof over your shipping container. This only takes a short amount of time to install, and provides better water run-off in case of precipitation.

Besides increased durability, a hip roof also offers other benefits:

- Harvesting rainwater
- Generating solar heat
- Additional natural light

If you are really considering going eco-friendly with your shipping container home and saving a lot on utilities, consider the benefits of having this installed in your roof to aid your solar power generation and rain water harvest.

***

These are just some of the things you will need to consider when planning the design of your shipping container home.

Simplify the planning and organization stages by recording everything and keeping track of your tasks and steps. If you like to use apps on your smartphone or tablet, consider using an organizational or task management app to aid you in planning your do-it-yourself shipping container home project.

Next up, we will cover where you can purchase the shipping container you are interested in.

7. Where To Purchase A Shipping Container

"I can say that the one thing that I wished I had not done was buy my containers without seeing them – I took the company's word that they would be in good shape. They were beat all to heck. The good thing was that most of the really dented places would end up being cut out of the containers anyway. And I wished I had known that it doesn't cost that much more for a One-Trip container and they are like brand new."

Larry Wade (Seacontainer Cabin), on what he would do differently now if he were to buy another shipping container and turn it into a home.

<u>**Key Takeaway**</u>: The steel container itself will be the main structure of your home, so it is crucial to select the best one you can get your hands on. There are used, slightly used, and brand new options, not to mention

the rise of prefabricated and ready-made container homes for even more convenience. Start your research online, and by asking family and friends. Before purchasing a container, inspect it in person. This is an absolute must if you are considering a used container. When you are satisfied, go ahead and place your order. Soon you are going to be the proud owner of a shipping container!

You now have a solid layout design in hand, and the right understanding of your:

- budget considerations
- available resources
- needed manpower, and
- other important aspects of the planning and organization stages of your project.

Your are finally ready for the purchase of the actual structure: the shipping container.

But where should you go to buy it?

***

Start Online

In this day and age of the Internet, most everything can be purchased online if you know where to look. Searching on popular commerce websites such as eBay.com and Craigslist.org will give you a first impression of the types of shipping containers that are for sale, and what they cost.

Here are some other websites that are worth checking out:

- Westerncontainersales.com
- Backcountrycontainers.com
- Shippingcontainers.net
- Carucontainers.com
- Shippingcontainersuk.com (UK)
- Portablespace.co.uk (UK)

For now, only use these websites to educate yourself on the different types of shipping containers that are on offer. Do not buy without inspection! You are not buying a pair of jeans on Amazon. This is likely going to be your home, and you do not want to buy a pig in a poke.

***

Ask Family and Friends

Next, talk to people you know you can trust. Do you have family members or friends who have already started or completed their own shipping container home repurposing? Connect with them and glean as much valuable information as you can, including:

- where they got their shipping container (and other materials)
- what they paid for it
- who they worked with, and
- what obstacles or struggles they have hurdled along the way

The input of your family or peers would be very beneficial to you at this stage, especially if you don't really know where to begin looking for new or used shipping containers to buy.

If family and friends cannot help you out, see if you can connect with any people in your community. They may be able to provide some real-world assistance regarding the purchase of a shipping container for residential reuse. This may include:

- contacts in shipping yards or port areas
- architects or design firms, or even
- your local city or town hall, that may be able to direct you to the right people.

You will be surprised about what information people you hardly know are willing to share, once they realize you are serious about joining the shipping container homes community.

***

Inspection: What to Look Out For?

Once you have a good understanding of what you want and can expect from a shipping container, it is time for the next step: physical inspection. At least, if you are considering buying a used shipping container. With new containers, you can safely assume that the container is delivered per your instructions. But with used containers you just don't really know until you see it with your own eyes. Think of it like this: *you are never going to know what chocolate cake tastes like if you only read books about it.* Similarly, you will only get a real feel for what to look for when buying a shipping container if you have seen, touched and smelled a few. In person.

Most used shipping containers are stored in or close to a port. In fact, the larger the metropolitan area and the closer it is to a large body of water used for international transport, the higher your chances will be of finding possible shipping container suppliers, let alone getting some great deals on these structures.

If you do not live in the vicinity of a port, you may consider skipping physical inspection to save yourself some money.

Do not make this mistake.

It is *absolutely crucial* that you inspect a container before purchase. After you have bought it and commenced building your home, there is no going back. And if your container starts to develop rust at a rapid speed shortly after you moved in, which you could have possibly prevented if you had inspection the container first. By then, you will probably want to punch yourself in the face.

Be smart. *Don't punch yourself in the face.*

If you really cannot do the inspection yourself, hire an expert to check out the container for you. Make sure he also takes photos – or even better: record a video – so you get the full picture when he reports his findings to you.

So what do you need to look out for when inspecting a shipping container?

- **CSC plate**: Every shipping container will have a so-called CSC plate on the door. This plate contains basic information about the container, such as the manufacturer, the production date, and for whom the container was built. This will give you an indication of how old the container is. A container that was manufactured 10 years ago has likely experienced more wear and tear than a younger one-trip container.
- **History**: Ask for the history of the container as this is readily available information. This way you will learn if it has been used for transporting agricultural products or livestock, and what kind of treatments or cleaning may be necessary to ensure that it will be safe for you to convert the container to a living space. In addition, you must also be aware of whether the container has been used for transporting other toxic substances or chemicals which would require additional solutions for treatment.

- **Doors**: Try opening and closing them. How do they feel? If they need a little push, that is not an immediate red flag. But if the alignment is off, that may indicate corrosion, which may then also be a concern elsewhere on the container. Also see if the doors swing open freely and if the locks work well.
- **Paint:** Some DIY shipping container home enthusiasts will advise you not to purchase a shipping container that has been repainted, especially if you smell fresh paint. The paint job may have been done to cover up any damage, rust, corrosion, or other imperfections that you should be aware of.
- **Dents:** Some minor wear and tear is to be expected on a shipping container. Serious dents are a cause for concern though.
- **Rust**: First closely examine the exterior and interior of the shipping container for damage such as flaking or paint chips. These could point to corrosion or rust underneath. Another method is one that works best on a sunny day. Close the doors after you have entered the container. It should be as dark as a black hole now. Do you see any light shining through? If

so, that is not a good sign: this could indicate deep rust, which is a no-go. However, a little bit of rust is no reason for concern. If you remember, shipping containers are coated with weathering or Corten steel, which forms a coating of rust-like oxidation to resist the corrosive effects of rain. When in doubt, consult an expert prior to purchasing a container.

- **Corten Steel**: Although most shipping containers are made with weathering steel, double check if this is the case for the one you are inspecting. Corten steel is much stronger than other types of steel and should you be your preferred building material.

***

The Moment is There: Let's Buy That Shipping Container!

After you have carefully inspected one or more shipping containers to your satisfaction, you are ready to pull the trigger and purchase the shipping container of your choosing.

When you purchase a shipping container, be sure to ask the seller whether the transport or delivery of the container is included in the purchase price. They may be able to negotiate a good price which includes transporting the container to your location, especially if you live far away ways from the port area where the shipping container will come from, or if the location where you want the shipping container to be delivered is not adjacent to the port area.

If you live inland or further from a shipping hub, there may be some hindrances to having the container shipped or transported to your area. If you are responsible for organizing transport, one option you may find effective is renting a large trailer truck or a truck with a tilting bed that can transport the container from the port or supplier. Be prepared to shell out more for transportation and/or shipping costs if you are not adjacent to a port area.

***

After all the preparatory work you have done, there is one final thing that can stand in the way of living in your shipping container home: passing the legal requirements in order to obtain a building permit. Let's look at that now.

8. Building Permit and Other Legal Requirements

"Every country has its own sets of rules and standards. This means a container house in the U.S. does not look like a container house in Denmark. That is something most people do not think about. The container is a generic product, but climate, fire regulations etc. are not..."

Mads Moller (Arcgency, a Danish Architectural office) on shipping container home regulations.

<u>Key Takeaway</u>: As with other types of housing construction, there are regulations covering the repurposing of shipping containers into homes. Your structure must comply with the general laws of the municipality you will be constructing in, and should *have the necessary permits before the project commences. Rules vary per region, so if you haven't picked a location yet, find one with lenient building code. If you are going to hire an architect or contractor, find one that is familiar with local building regulations. Communicate openly during the application process, submit all the necessary paperwork and address any concerns. This will maximize your chances of success!*

One of the biggest concerns for future container homeowners is obtaining a building permit. Unfortunately, there is no 'one-size-fits-all' set of criteria that, when followed, will always result in a building permit being granted. However, if you spend some time researching and understanding the legal requirements before you apply, you can greatly increase your chances of checking all the boxes and receiving the 'go-ahead'.

***

What is a Building Code?

A building code is a set of regulations that contain the minimum requirements for the construction, design and maintenance of buildings. These rules aim to protect the health and safety of the occupants of the building. Compliance with them is mandatory in order to receive a permit.

***

Rules Vary Per Region

Wouldn't it be great if there was one building code, that would apply to all buildings nationwide?

If only life was that simple…

Unfortunately, in the United States the building codes and regulations vary for every city, municipality, and state. So what applies to someone looking to build a home in Topeka, Kansas may not necessarily be required for someone erecting a residential structure in Fort Lauderdale, Florida.

This is why it is important to check with your local city, town, or municipal authorities regarding requirements, necessary permits, building codes, and other regulations before you even begin constructing anything. Zoning restrictions are also crucial, so before finalizing a location, make sure you will be allowed to construct your project in your desired area first.

***

Research Different Locations

You may even look into building your shipping container home in an area that has no building codes, or with very little regulations, that is if you have not yet made any final decision on the location or purchased any land. There are still some districts or locations in the United States with lenient or no building codes, and you may find it easier to construct your shipping container home project in one of these areas.

Here are some towns and counties in the United States with little to no building codes and regulations, allowing you more freedom to design your living space:

- Marfa, Texas
- The Field Lab, Terlingua, Texas
- Delta County, Colorado
- Earthship Biotecture, New Mexico

The downside to building in a county or town with little to no building codes is the limited access to services and conveniences which you may already be accustomed to, such as utility providers for water, electricity, or gas, and proximity to supermarkets, schools, and other retailers. Cellular phone, landline, or Internet access may also be more difficult to attain in these areas because they are typically far from major population centers.

If you are building in a more populated county, it would be wise to have all your building documents ready before applying for permits. This way, any questions that local authorities may have regarding your shipping container home project can be more easily answered with the visual help of your blueprints and plans. For the design itself, the building commissioner in your area would issue the permit prior to any other codes or licenses.

***

Hire a Local Architect

It would be best to hire the services of a qualified professional architect or engineer with the knowledge of building regulations in your specific county or city, so they can integrate regulations into every aspect of your design prior to seeking approval. An architectural firm or designer from a different state may not be as well-versed in the local regulations you will need to satisfy.

***

Prepare all the Paperwork

Get a good understanding of all the paperwork that you will need to submit during the application process.

An important requirement is that you will probably be faced with is presenting technical drawings of the shipping container or containers you will be using for the construction. This is often needed so authorities can ascertain the structural integrity of the container you will be using. A physical evaluation of the container may even be required, so to make the process go smoother make sure you have all of this documentation from the supplier when you purchase.

Regulations and requirements may be less stressful if you will be purchasing prefabricated shipping container homes from manufacturers, especially if it is with a locally-based manufacturer with knowledge and experience in the local jurisdiction you will be building on. However, there are not many of these manufacturers yet, so do your due diligence and connect with the proper channels first before making any major decisions regarding your shipping container home project.

***

Address Specific Concerns Regarding Shipping Containers

For the most part, the building regulations and permits for shipping container homes are the same as those for traditional housing projects.

At first glance, one would expect that shipping container homes would be embraced by local governments. They are much sturdier than a trailer home. And they even score points when compared to traditional houses, especially when it comes to being able to withstand bad weather conditions.

However, there are a few possible concerns that you may need to address during the application process. A lot of people, including neighbors and government officials involved in the building permit application process, are unfamiliar with shipping container homes. They may oppose it for different reasons.

Neighbors may fear that a giant steel container next door may negatively impact their property value. And inspectors or surveyors may give you a hard time before any permits are issued because they are concerned about a lack of proper insulation or fortifications.

Anticipate these concerns and come up with a plan on how you are going to address them. *Well begun is half done.*

One tip: it may be a good idea to do some research in your locality and find out if there are existing shipping container homes already constructed, or even retail or office spaces converted from shipping containers. If you are able to locate some in your general area, just knock on the door and ask if you can have a chat with the owner. Voice your concerns, and ask about their experience.

The owner of this shipping container home has successfully gone through the permit application process. You may be able to get some valuable information or leads on what requirements you will need to satisfy, or what permits to acquire, before building.

The occupant of this home would be an excellent person to talk to.

***

Communicate Openly

Clear communication with the people involved in the permit application process is a key factor, and having all your layouts or plans ready should be imperative.

You must get the message across that what you will be constructing is not just a gigantic steel box with squalid living conditions inside, but rather a residential structure repurposed from what is considered one of the most durable building materials to date.

***

After all the construction and prior to moving in, a building inspector will make a final check of the finished structure and clear it with existing regulations, as well as certificate of occupancy. Be transparent and truthful at all times and submit all necessary paperwork in order to more efficiently smooth the process along. It would be better for your project in general if no shortcuts are made along the way. Rather, each step must be meticulously attended to to ensure clearance with local regulators.

9. Final Considerations

"Shipping containers are like my favorite people. Overall, they are very simple, but they have intense bits of complexity. Knowing and understanding those complexities is truly key to being successful with a container build."

Katie Nichols (Numen Development), on building the Cordell house with shipping containers.

<u>**Key Takeaway**</u>: It may seem overwhelming at first, but your shipping container home project will be well worth the satisfaction you will feel as you see the results. Let's wrap this book up with a few final things to consider: some thoughts on eco-friendly living, planning for family growth, downsizing, and joining the shipping container homes community.

You now know all the basics of creating your shipping container home. I hope by now you are really excited to take action, and make your container home dream come true!

Here are a few last things to consider to ensure that you will enjoy your new home long-term.

***

Living in an Eco-Friendly Way

In opting for a shipping container home, you are afforded a more sustainable, eco-friendly housing option that is at the forefront of environmentally-mindful efforts to reuse or repurpose available resources and reduce wastage. With this goal in mind, you would do well to be aware and mindful of other ways to maximize available and renewable resources for your container home's other needs, as well as an overall sustainable way of life.

For example, shipping container homes can potentially be fitted with solar panels in order to generate the required electricity to power lighting and other appliances. Check out available tax deductions or government incentives in your area for solar power generation. This option has become increasingly affordable for homeowners and supported by many local jurisdictions, so you may be able to save more if utilizing solar power for your shipping container home.

***

Family

As you plan your container home project, be mindful of how this can potentially impact your daily way of life, as well as your short-term or long-term plans. Are you planning to start – or further grow – a family? The design should be flexible enough to allow for additional room, for instance if you expect to have more children in the future and need to expand. Fortunately, shipping container homes afford flexibility in expansion designs.

What changes will you need to make as far as personal belongings or conveniences? Depending on your current living situation, you may need to downsize or reduce furniture, fixtures, and other modern conveniences in order to comfortably inhabit your shipping container home. This may even have a positive impact on your purchasing habits, as you become more mindful of the space limitations and make wiser choices on things you will be buying in the future.

***

Downsizing

If downsizing is a necessity, consider selling items of clothing, personal accessories, home appliances and devices, and other junk you may have accumulated over the years, and using the additional money towards your shipping container home project. You can even consider donating other items in good condition to local charitable organizations which can put them to good use, or directing any financial proceeds towards environmental causes you may have discovered as you research on your container home plans.

***

Join the Community

Connecting with other shipping container home enthusiasts and builders would be advantageous to you both *during* the project and even *well beyond* the completion of your new home. New innovations, ideas, and concepts are continually being discovered and tested by the container home community, and you should always be open to learning new things and applying them to your own endeavors.

The project does not end once your shipping container home is erected and you have finally moved in. In fact, this will just be the beginning of your new adventure. Maintenance, improvements, and challenges will continually test your resolve and add to your knowledge on the subject, so networking with other like-minded individuals from your community and around the world will expose you to ideas that could benefit you in the long run.

One of your goals should also be to share best practices and valuable experiences with the community. As you find how convenient, sustainable, and satisfying it is to inhabit a repurposed shipping container space, your insights and lessons could be invaluable to others who are also interested in taking on this journey for themselves. Just as you were able to glean useful information from others as you were starting out, you should also be willing to pass along that information to future seekers and builders.

The movement of repurposing shipping containers into homes and other building structures is just beginning to take hold and capture the attention of individuals and families across the globe. As the idea becomes more mainstream and increasingly accepted and even encouraged in communities and jurisdictions, expect to see more innovative concepts that aim to reduce the impact of these steel containers on our already pressured environment.

Perhaps, in the near future, we will see a transformation in the general attitude of the global community towards sustainable housing and recycling efforts, and more emphasis will be placed on reusing what resources are already available with the hopes of minimizing waste. As you decide how to proceed with your shipping container home project, remember that you are also helping to be a part of history and the continued emphasis on conservation.

Undoubtedly, there will also be an impact on future generations, and you need not go far to assess the positive impact you can create. If you have children and they have a pleasant experience living in a reused shipping container home, they will very likely imbibe these lessons and carry them on to adulthood. Perhaps, you will also see them seek to carry out the same projects later on and try to replicate what you have accomplished.

Our decisions, no matter how small or big they may seem at the moment, have an impact far beyond what we can see presently. Be conscious of this responsibility as you consider a shipping container home and how it can be a positive example to your family, your sphere of influence, and your community at large. How many people may be inspired to make conscious changes in their lifestyles and conservation efforts if you set a good precedent?

This may seem like just a shipping container home project to consider, but the impact can be far-reaching, so make the right choices and be as informed as you can, knowing that you are building not just a home, but a future.

Conclusion

There you have it: the keys to the castle!

Thank you so much for taking the time to read this book, *'Shipping Container Homes: Learn How To Build Your Own Shipping Container House and Live Your Dream!'*

You should now have a good understanding of what it takes to build a shipping container home, and be able to make an informed decision on whether this is the right option for you.

You have learned:

- What shipping container homes are
- The benefits of shipping container homes
- What to consider before purchasing one
- How to choose a shipping container that is right for you
- How to take the necessary safety precautions

- The basics of designing a shipping container home
- Where to purchase a shipping container home, and
- How you can maximize your chances during the permit application process

The next step is to apply what you have learned. This can be a challenging process at times. We all have our moments of weakness. Take it one step at a time. And don't beat yourself up if you temporarily fall off track. Nobody is perfect! Success is simply a matter of getting up one more time than you fall.

I wish you success on your journey, and I hope you feel a deep sense of satisfaction once you move into your shipping container home for the first time. Can you see yourself sitting there, with a glass of wine and some candles on, taking in the moment?

***

Finally, if you enjoyed this Tiny Living book bundle (RV Living & Shipping Container Homes), I would like to ask you for a favor. Would you be kind enough to share your thoughts and post a review of this book online? Just a few sentences would already be really helpful.

Your voice is important for this book to reach as many people as possible.

The more reviews this book gets, the more people will be able to find it and enjoy the incredible benefits of living in an RV or shipping container home.

Thank you again for reading this book and good luck with applying what you have learned!

About The Author

From a young age, I have always loved living life off the grid. What started small, with climbing trees and exploring the outdoors, developed into a profound interest in anything that would not confine me to the standard '9-5 get a mortgage' kinda lifestyle.

I wanted to experience real freedom. Without having to spend a fortune.

That's when I took a leap of faith, bought my first RV, and traveled across the country. It was not always easy, but I learned how to support myself on the way, and eventually created the lifestyle I always dreamed of.

Once I decided to settle down for a while, I built my own shipping container home. Did you know you can buy one at the fraction of the cost of a traditional home?

This lifestyle is not as difficult to reach as you may think. The most important thing is that you take action, one step at a time. I want to help you access that freedom, so you too can turn your dreams into reality!

www.ingramcontent.com/pod-product-compliance
Lightning Source LLC
Chambersburg PA
CBHW072002110526
44592CB00012B/1180